Piece AND Quilt
As You Go

Dedication

Thank you to my husband, Jaime. His encouragement, patience,
and crazy antics get me through the challenging design
moments. He doesn't let a disheveled home, fast food meals,
and lack of fresh laundry during deadlines upset him.

Piece and Quilt As You Go

Landauer Publishing, www.landauerpub.com, is an imprint of Fox Chapel Publishing Company, Inc.

Copyright © 2024 by Debi Schmitz Noriega and Fox Chapel Publishing Company, Inc.

Project Team
Managing Editor: Gretchen Bacon
Acquisitions Editor: Amelia Johanson
Editor: Christa Oestreich
Designer: Wendy Reynolds
Studio Photographer: Mike Mihalo
Illustrations: Sue Friend
Proofreader & Indexer: Jean Bissell

Shutterstock used: John M. Chase (9), Steve Bower (10), jafara (53 background), David Papazian (59 and 66 background), vanitjan (73 and 88 background), FotoDuets (81 baby and background), Pixel-Shot (93 background), Fascinadora (101 background), I love photo (111 background), New Africa (121 background), Dolores M. Harvey (125 background), Liderina (127 and 131 photos), archideaphoto (133 background).

ISBN 978-1-63981-071-0

Library of Congress Control Number: 2024940353

To learn more about the other great books from Fox Chapel Publishing, or to find a retailer near you, call toll-free 800-457-9112, send mail to 903 Square Street, Mount Joy, PA 17552, or visit us at www. FoxChapelPublishing.com.

We are always looking for talented authors. To submit an idea, please send a brief inquiry to acquisitions@foxchapelpublishing.com.

Note to Professional Copy Services:
The publisher grants you permission to make up to six copies of any quilt patterns in this book for any customer who purchased this book and states the copies are for personal use.

Printed in China
First printing

Piece AND Quilt As You Go

Techniques, Tips, and 24 Modern Designs Simplified

Debi Schmitz Noriega

Landauer Publishing

Contents

24

28

32

38

42

48

52

58

62

66

72

76

80

88

92

96

What Does it Mean to Quilt As You Go?

What is Quilt As You Go (QAYG)? It's a technique of quilting one block—top, batting, and backing fabric—at one time. This group of three is often referred to as a quilt sandwich. Once the blocks are pieced and quilted, the project blocks are joined.

Quilters also call Quilt As You Go a "stitch-and-flip" method because, after stitching a strip of fabric, it will be flipped back, and the seam is pressed before proceeding to the next fabric strip; ironing and squaring up blocks between each step is the key. This is a straightforward way to complete quilted projects rapidly.

By completing all layers as you go, at the end of the block completion and the joining of the blocks, you are finished except for the binding! This technique is fantastic for table runners, pillows, book covers, lap quilts, and wall quilts. Any size quilt can be completed with these techniques.

Quilting a design on a traditionally pieced project with a home sewing machine is a struggle, much like dressing a toddler that will not sit still. There is a lot of twisting, turning, scrunching, pushing, and pulling. During the fight, stitches often needed to be ripped out and replaced with more polished stitching. In many cases, the amount of aggravation does not seem worth it.

Many quilters will therefore take the pieced quilt top, batting, and backing fabric to a long-arm-machine owner for the actual quilting. These machines are exceptionally large and can accommodate sizeable projects. With the touch of a button, the machine will follow programmed software to stitch a chosen design in no time. However, it can be expensive, and few have the space and budget for their own long arm.

Let's look at the benefits of QAYG:

- **Small blocks.** Instead of finishing a giant quilt top, you are finishing each block separately. By completing all layers as you go, all that's left is the binding! It also does not require much space to QAYG because you are working on one block at a time.
- **Quick and simple.** This is a straightforward way to complete quilted projects rapidly. You can use a standard sewing machine—nothing fancy required. It's also a technique that is easy to teach to younger generations with few boundaries.
- **Budget-friendly.** You only need small pieces, which could mean using up those leftover scraps and blocks. I usually purchase more fabric than required, so I do not have to worry about it being discontinued mid project. Keep in mind that fabrics change quite often in stores unless they are a bestseller. Also, multiple trips to the quilt store can adversely affect the project budget.
- **Use recycled fabric.** QAYG is great for memory quilts. Just after my father passed away, we searched for easy projects to make that used his old shirts. QAYG is a great option to complete lap quilts or pillows for everyone in the family in little time.
- **Little waste.** Using scraps of fabric or recycled fabric in new quilting projects helps our environment. Quilts are passed from generation to generation, so there is not much chance of finding them in your local landfill.

My slogan is the following: **There are no mistakes. These are called character flaws and can be a unique part of your work.**

Keep calm and enjoy the process.

This quilt is made much more manageable by finishing each square and rectangle first, then joining them together.

Tools and Materials

When purchasing your tools and materials, keep your budget in mind as well as the quality of the tools and materials. There are many outlets for products these days, but shopping at a qualified quilt store or fabric store will be very beneficial. Tools should be durable and be kept in a place for sewing tools only. Materials will range in quality. For most of these projects, you don't need to purchase the highest quality, but choose an adequate quality for longevity and use.

Notes About Thread

I like to use Coats Dual Duty threads, although there are lots of options available to quilters. I have tried other threads, and this is just at my comfort level. Things to take into consideration when purchasing thread for your sewing machine:

- **Read the instructions** with your sewing machine and follow its guidance.
- **"All purpose" is safe** for most sewing projects. It is often a cotton blend.
- **Use strong thread.** Keep in mind that you will be sewing through several layers of fabrics and batting when doing Quilt As You Go.
- **A cotton or polycotton blend** is usually the best thread for this type of quilting.
- **Evaluate threads on scraps** of fabric before and during the quilting process. Scraps of fabric are perfect for testing tension, stitch appearance, and the quality of the thread. These scraps are also useful for beginning and ending stitches of seams.
- **Keep care instructions in mind** for the fabric, batting, and thread. They need to be compatible.
- **Keep the threads clipped** throughout the project to keep them out of the seams.

Notes About Batting

I love working with Warm & Natural Needled Cotton Batting, but I did use Poly-Fil Extra-Loft® for two of the designs in this book for a deeper quilting look. There are many different batting choices, so let me break it down a little.

- **Cotton batting** is lightweight and breathes well. I prefer needle-punched batting because it is felted with thousands of needle punches, so it holds together and does not pull apart easily.
- **Microwave batting** is fun when making trivets, coffee mug mats, bread covers, and casserole wraps. Be sure to read all manufacturer's instructions before using.
- **Fusible batting** is a great alternative if you are worried about movement of your fabric pieces when quilting. I prefer to use basting spray as needed.
- **Polyester batting** is thicker, but lighter weight. It does not breathe well but is usually warmer.

Standard Batting Sizes

Craft	36" x 45" (91.4 x 114.3cm)
Crib	45" x 60" (114.3 x 152.4cm)
Throw	50" x 65" (127 x 165.1cm)
Twin	72" x 90" (182.9 x 228.6cm)
Full	81" x 96" (205.7 x 243.8cm)
Queen	90" x 108" (228.6 x 274.3cm)
King	120" x 120" (304.8 x 304.8cm)

- **Wool batting** is lightweight and very warm. Another wonderful thing about wool batting is that it never shows creases or folds.
- **Bamboo batting** is a blend of 50% bamboo and 50% organic cotton. This batting is "green," meaning it is processed using pollution-free techniques. Bamboo is more expensive, but it drapes beautifully and dries quickly after washing. This is a great batting for an heirloom project.
- **Test your battings** for the appropriate iron temperature. Use a pressing cloth if necessary.

I watch for coupons and sales to buy my batting, and then I buy enough for several projects. I love having it on hand. There is nothing worse than sitting down to a new Quilt As You Go project and finding that you do not have enough batting. You need the batting from start to finish when doing QAYG.

Notes About Fabrics

I prefer cotton fabrics but have also used cotton/poly blends in this book. There is something beautiful in the feel of quality cotton.

- **Cotton** is tightly woven, easy to cut and sew, durable, and breathable. This fabric is the most popular among quilters.
- **Batik** is handmade and dyed to be great for adding color and texture to a project.
- **Flannel** is a cozy alternative for baby gifts and lap quilts in chilly weather climates.
- **Linen** is used for an elegant appearance, but it has many characteristics to consider like washability and strength.
- **The fabrics in this book are 44"–45" (111.8–114.3cm) wide.** If using different widths, keep this in mind when purchasing the fabrics and adjust accordingly.
- **Keep track of the laundering instructions** for the fabrics you choose. Make sure they are compatible. Test scraps for appropriate iron temperature.

- **Cut conservatively** from one end to the other when cutting fabrics. Never waste fabric by cutting from the center.
- **When sewing with a directional pattern fabric**, be mindful of the front and back as you create.
- **Keep a swatch for sewing.** I like to have a swatch of fabric that I can start the needle in and then stitch on the fabrics on which I am working. I use another swatch at the other end of the seam to end the threads.

I have made every attempt to provide the correct amounts of fabric needed for the projects, but keep in mind that every cutting mistake will change the amount of fabric needed. When buying fabrics, I **always** buy a little more, or I will be in and out of the quilt store more than the employees. Another reason to purchase a little more than requested is that you will get the same dye lot. Like yarns, fabrics can differ in different dye lots.

I have found that the best-quality fabrics are found in local quilt shops. They purchase their inventory from professional fabric manufacturers that take color, strength, durability, feel, and appearance into consideration. These days, fabric is made at several quality levels, and you need to be careful to choose wisely. Your local quilt shop will direct you to the best for the project you have in mind.

Needed Tools

- **Rotary Cutter and Extra Blades**—I would be lost without my rotary cutter. You may create all the projects in this book with simple fabric scissors, but why? If you have not tried a rotary cutter, give it a whirl. You will be so glad you did!
- **Cutting Mat**—This is a companion to the rotary cutter and comes in all sizes and colors. Choose what speaks to you. Mine is a basic one that is dark gray on one side and light gray on the other so I can flip it with different fabric colors in mind.
- **Acrylic Ruler**—Another companion of the rotary cutter. I love using a clear acrylic ruler that allows me to see what I am working with under it. The rotary cutter glides along the edge without bubbling or cutting the end of my finger off.
- **Thin, Sharp Quilting Pins**—I used to pick up the cheapest pins I could find for work in my studio. Let us not do that. I discovered that by using high-quality quilting pins, I get much better results and they do not all end up in the garbage because they bend.

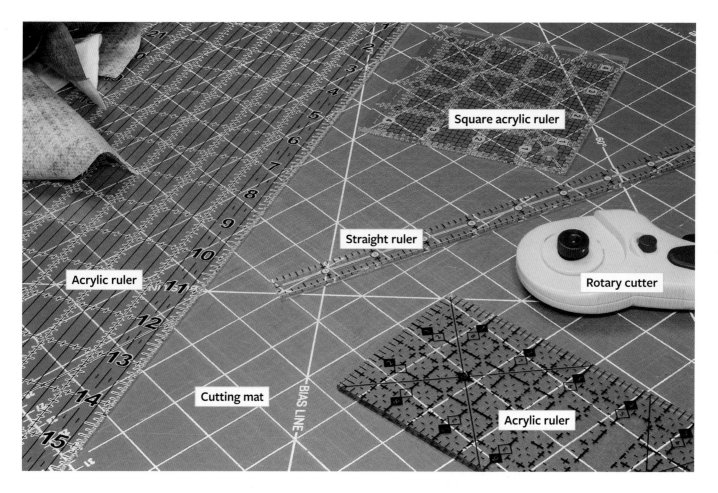

Square acrylic ruler

Straight ruler

Rotary cutter

Acrylic ruler

Cutting mat

BIAS LINE

Acrylic ruler

- **Fabric Scissors**—Have special fabric scissors in your possession, and lock them up when you are not using them—unless you live alone. I am serious.
- **Seam Ripper**—This is one of my best friends. I find myself ripping seams all the time. Keep a sharp one that fits in your hand comfortably next to your workstation.
- **Portable or Regular-Size Ironing Board and Iron**—I use both. My large iron and ironing board are great for large projects, but I love my wool ironing mat. It might smell like a wet sheep, but it works wonderfully.
- **Sewing Machine**—I love my Brother Pacesetter PS500. That is just me. When purchasing a sewing machine, do not go out and buy the cheapest or buy the expensive one that does everything including your nails. Talk to several different quilters, store owners, and friends that sew. Also read reviews and recommendations of reputable outlets.

  Make sure that you have a machine in fantastic working order and up to date on maintenance. There is nothing worse than being ready to dive into a new project, and instead, ending up fighting with your machine. **Keep your machine clean!** Follow your manufacturer's instructions and follow scheduled maintenance.

- **Extra Needles for Piecing and Quilting**—Ask for the right needles for the job.

OTHER RECOMMENDED TOOLS
- **Fabric Basting Spray**—I love this for a quick hold before sewing. Be sure to read all manufacturer's instructions before using.
- **Iron-On Adhesive**—This is a paper-feel product that has iron-on adhesive on one side. It is to be ironed to a piece of fabric, then that fabric is ironed to another like appliqué.
- **Iron-On Adhesive Tape**—This is an iron-on adhesive that is provided in a narrow strip, such as ½" (1.3cm). It is ironed to one fabric, and when ironed to another fabric, it creates a bond.
- **Walking Foot**—Just discovered this recently. Why was I not told sooner? This foot is fantastic when you are sewing through multiple layers of fabrics.
- **Zipper Foot**—When attaching an invisible zipper, you will need an invisible zipper foot to allow the seam to be close to the zipper teeth.
- **Quarter-Inch Sewing Machine Foot**—When I started sewing, a long, long time ago, I was told that the presser foot will stitch a perfect ¼" (6.4mm) seam. Not anymore—look at your sewing machine tool kit. There are so many different ones and sizes.

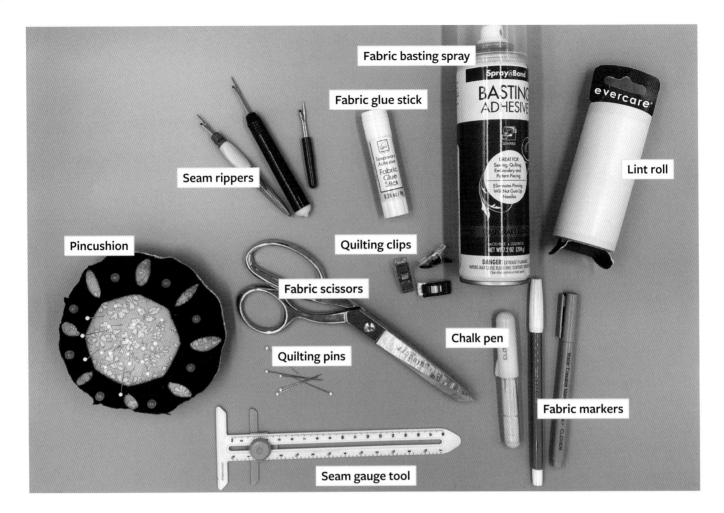

Fabric basting spray

Fabric glue stick

Lint roll

Seam rippers

Pincushion

Quilting clips

Fabric scissors

Chalk pen

Quilting pins

Fabric markers

Seam gauge tool

- **Seam Gauge Tool**—I love this tool. I have written several books with my sidekick, the seam gauge tool. It is the best for measuring small seams, stitches, or scraps of fabric.
- **Tear-Away Stabilizer**—Just a enough for backing the end of the tail appliqué for the Lemur Play Mat (page 80).

OPTIONAL TOOLS

- **Quilting Clips**—I love these for some applications, but I use the sharp quilting pins more. These would be safer for me.
- **Lint Brush or Roll**—Not only do I live in a house with pets, but I cannot stand all the tiny threads that collect on my projects and workspace. A lint roll is perfect for capturing all those cut threads. Also, when you rip out seams, this helps to remove that loose thread.
- **Chalk Pen or Fabric Marker**—I always have a pencil, pen, chalk pen, or fabric marker in my toolbox. If nothing else, I can add to the grocery list next to me.
- **Fabric Glue Stick**—This is a great tool for installing an invisible zipper. It helps by holding pieces of fabric until you have a chance to stitch them.

- **Pressing Spray**—Love this. There is nothing like sewing pressed, firm fabrics. I just love the feel of the fabric in the sewing machine when it is not creased or holding fold lines.
- **Awl or Blunt-Point Instrument**—An awl isn't necessarily blunt, but whatever is chosen should help ease the fabric into the corners of a pillow without damaging the fabric.
- **Pincushion or Container for Pins**—If you are like me, this is a necessity; otherwise, you will find yourself sitting on or stepping on those fantastic quilting pins. You do not want that.
- **Needles and Strong Thread (Hand Sewing)**—There is usually a little hand sewing required when quilting. Keep your spools available, orderly, and visible.
- **Freezer Paper**—This will protect the work surface when using basting spray. You can also use newspaper, copy paper, or paper towel.
- **Bias-Tape Maker**—Small metal or plastic tool. It folds the fabric strip in half as it is pulled through.
- **Grommet Template**—Grommet templates are clear pieces of plastic that have openings to draw through to mark the opening on the fabric. They come with the grommets.

Joining Techniques

In this section, I will explain several different joining techniques for Quilt As You Go. Remember, the basis of Quilt As You Go (QAYG) is to complete the blocks with the fabric, batting, and in most cases, the backing fabrics at the same time, so joining them is the only step left to complete the project.

There is a variety of different techniques and methods for joining the completed blocks, but in my research, the ones listed here are the top five. There are techniques that join the batting between the blocks and others that use decorative stitches on top to connect the blocks. I suggest trying them all and then choosing the one with which you are most comfortable. The finished project design might dictate which technique you use.

Technique 1— QAYG with Separate Backing

In this technique, the batting and pieced front will be the same size. Piece the block on the batting; when complete, add the backing fabric. To quilt the block, "stitch-in-the-ditch" from the front. Additional quilting may be added but is not necessary. All seams are ¼" (6.4mm) unless otherwise noted.

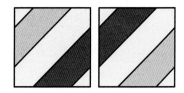

1. Piece the block according to the project pattern, stitching through the batting at the same time. Stitch to the edges of the batting. Flip each added fabric piece back to the batting after stitching, and press the seam. Complete all blocks. Square up the blocks. All blocks will be square and the same size unless otherwise noted in the pattern.

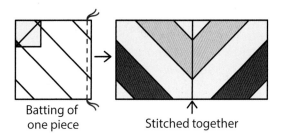

Batting of one piece   Stitched together

2. Attach two side-by-side blocks by stitching together along one edge with right sides together. Be sure that the front and the back of the blocks are positioned correctly for the finished project. Iron the seam open.

3. Connect all blocks for a row, matching seams and sides. Repeat for all rows. Press seams. Connect the rows. Be sure to match all seams.

Terms to Know

Piece	Construct.
Right Side	Front of block or fabric.
Square Up	Make sure that the sides are all straight, square to each other, and trimmed. This is where the cutting mat, acrylic ruler, and rotary cutter are indispensable.
Stitch-in-the-Ditch	Stitch in the same stitch lines from the front to add the quilting stitches to the back.
Wrong Side	Back of the block or fabric.

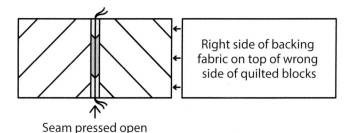

Right side of backing fabric on top of wrong side of quilted blocks

Seam pressed open

4. When the front of the quilt is finished, add the quilt back. Trim the front and back to the same size. Use basting spray to hold the backing in place. On the front, stitch-in-the-ditch so the same quilted design is on the back of the block. The quilt back will be attached wrong side down on the batting. Finish the project with a bias edging (page 16).

Tip

If using basting spray, protect your work surface with parchment paper or something similar.

Technique 2—
QAYG with Narrow Front Strip

In this technique, piece the block front, batting, and backing fabric at the same time. All three are the same size. Only stitch ¼"–½" (0.6–1.3cm) from the outside edge of the batting. The blocks will be attached with a **narrow front strip** and a wider back strip. Since you are quilting the block as you complete, there is no need for additional quilting. All seam allowances are ¼" (6.4mm) unless noted.

← Stitch seams ½" from outside edge

1. Piece the block according to the project pattern, stitching through the three layers at the same time. Sew to ½" (1.3cm) from the outside edge of the block. If blocks are smaller than 8" (20.3cm), quilt to ¼" (6.4mm) from the outside edge. Press seams after each piece is added. Complete all blocks. Square up the blocks.

2. Quilt the blocks according to the pattern or as desired, again up to ½" (1.3cm) from the outside edge.

← FOLD

Fold 2" strip lengthwise and press the fold.

3. Cut a 2" (5.1cm) strip and a 1" (2.5cm) strip of fabric. These strips should be slightly longer than the block's edge. Fold the 2" (5.1cm) wide strip of fabric in half lengthwise (1" [2.5cm] x length) wrong sides together.

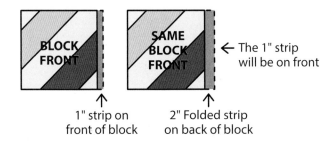

← The 1" strip will be on front

1" strip on front of block

2" Folded strip on back of block

4. Place the folded 2" (5.1cm) strip on the back of the block. Place the 1" (2.5cm) strip on the front of the block, right sides together, with the raw edges lined up to the same block edge. Sew through the top strip, block, and bottom strip at the same time.

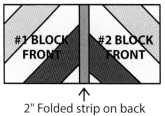

2" Folded strip on back

5. Fold the 2" (5.1cm) strip over. Place the second block on the other edge of the strip, right sides together, and join. Fold flat and press flat.

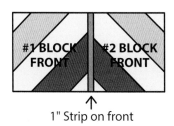

1" Strip on front

6. Fold the 1" (2.5cm) strip over, so it is on the second block. Stitch down. This stitch line will show on the back, so be aware of placement. This step can be hand sewn as well. Use this technique to attach all blocks in a row.

7. To attach the rows together, use 1" (2.5cm) and 2" (5.1cm) strips that are slightly longer than the row.

Technique 3—
QAYG with Wide Front Strip

In this technique, piece the block front, batting, and backing at the same time. All three are the same size. The blocks will be attached with a **wide front strip** on the front and a narrow back strip. Since you are quilting the block as you complete, there is no need for additional quilting. All seams will be ¼" (6.4mm) unless noted.

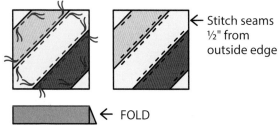

← Stitch seams ½" from outside edge

← FOLD

Fold 2" strip lengthwise and press the fold.

1. Follow steps 1–3 of Technique 2.

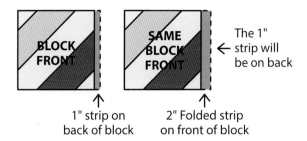

1" strip on
back of block

2" Folded strip
on front of block

The 1"
← strip will
be on back

2. Place the 1" (2.5cm) strip on the back of the block, wrong side down. Place the 2" (5.1cm) strip on the front of the block, right sides together, with the raw edges lined up to the same block edge. Sew through the top strip, block, and bottom strip at the same time with ¼" (6.4mm) seam.

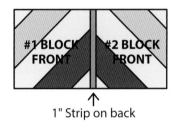

1" Strip on back

3. Fold the 1" (2.5cm) strip over, so it is right side up. Place the second block on the other edge of the strip, right sides together, and join. Fold flat and press flat.

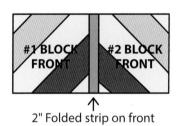

2" Folded strip on front

4. Fold the 2" (5.1cm) strip over, so it is right side up on the second block. Stitch down. This stitch line will show on the back, so be aware of placement. This step can be hand sewn as well. Use this technique to attach all blocks in a row.

5. To attach the rows together, use 1" (2.5cm) and 2" (5.1cm) strips that are slightly longer than the row.

Technique 4—
QAYG with Front Binding

In this technique, piece the block front, batting, and backing at the same time. All three are the same size. Blocks will be attached by stitching the backing sides together, ironing the seams flat, and then stitching an open bias tape over the seams on the front. All seams are ¼" (6.4mm) unless noted.

1. Piece the block according to the project pattern, stitching through the three layers at the same time. Sew to the edges. Press all seams open.

2. Complete all blocks. Square up the blocks. All blocks will be the same size and squared unless otherwise noted. Quilt the blocks according to the pattern or as desired.

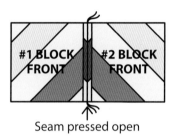

Seam pressed open

3. Sew two finished blocks, wrong sides together, so the seam is on the front of the blocks.

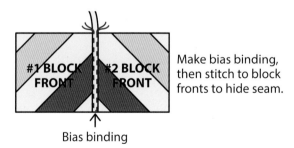

Bias binding

Make bias binding, then stitch to block fronts to hide seam.

4. Make bias tape (page 16) with the fabric strips in the pattern. Attach iron-on adhesive tape to the back of the bias tape. Press to the seam of the blocks. Hand stitch or machine sew the bias tape in place near both edges.

Technique 5— QAYG Framing Technique

In this technique, cut the backing fabric wider than the batting and pieced front by 2" (5.1cm) in each dimension. For example, a 10" x 10" (25.4 x 25.4cm) pieced front will need a 12" x 12" (30.5 x 30.5cm) backing. Adjustments to this might be necessary if working with smaller finished blocks. The front and the batting will be the same size as the finished block. Join the blocks, wrong sides together, close to the blocks, and then fold the excess fabric around to frame the blocks.

 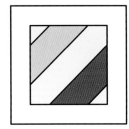

Cut fabric 2" larger all around

1. Spray the piece of batting with basting spray. Place it in the center of the backing fabric, sticky side to wrong side of backing. Piece your block according to the project pattern, stitching through the three layers at the same time. Stitch to the edges of the block. Press the seams open.

2. Complete all blocks. Square up the blocks after piecing is finished. All blocks will be squared and the same size unless otherwise noted. Quilt the blocks according to the pattern or as desired.

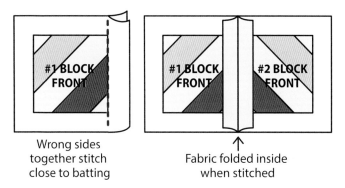

Wrong sides together stitch close to batting

Fabric folded inside when stitched

3. Join the blocks, right sides of backings together. Sew as close to the edge of the batting as possible. Open the blocks. The interior edges of the backing fabric are now fanned out like the pages of a book. Press the seam open.

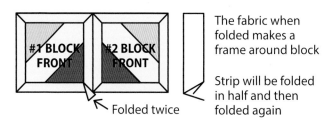

The fabric when folded makes a frame around block

Strip will be folded in half and then folded again

Folded twice

4. Fold the raw edge of one "page" under, like making bias tape. Fold over again so the raw edge is hidden inside. Repeat for all sides, stitching along the folded edge. All corners should be sewn like binding a quilt. Complete a row of blocks, and repeat for all rows.

5. Attach all rows the same way, matching all seams. The framing technique finishes the edges of the quilt, no other binding is necessary.

Finishing Techniques

Please keep in mind that throughout this book I am using basic or beginner techniques and terms. When quilt making, I occasionally make mistakes just like you. Don't panic—everything can be fixed in one way or another. You will discover that you can complete all these projects and so many more if you relax and enjoy the process. I am not a professional quilter; I have a huge imagination and a love for new creative projects, and I love teaching. Many of my stitches are less than perfect. Enjoy the process of choosing fabrics, threads, battings, and embellishments. Each step is fulfilling!

Half-Inch Double-Fold Bias Tape

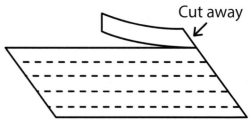

3. Draw lines 2" (5.1cm) apart from the bottom to the top of the fabric piece as shown. Cut off the excess fabric that is not a full 2" (5.1cm).

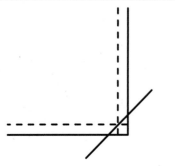

1. Cut the square of fabric across a corner, diagonally, for two triangular pieces.

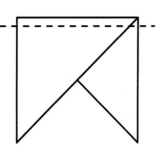

2. With right sides together and using a ¼" (6.4mm) seam allowance, sew the triangles together along one edge as shown. Press the seam allowance open.

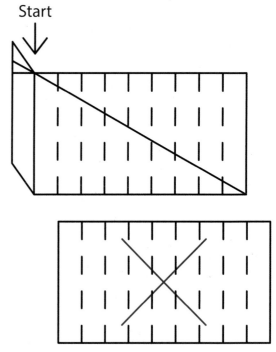

4. With the right sides on the inside, bring short edges together to form a tube. Offset the lines by one strip. **Do not line it up evenly.** Pin edges together by inserting pins ¼" (6.4mm) from cut edges through drawn lines. The lines should intersect at this ¼" (6.4mm) point. Sew edges together using a ¼" (6.4mm) seam allowance, and press open.

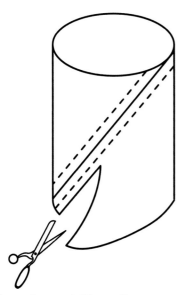

5. Cut along the pencil lines for a continuous 2" (5.1cm) strip of fabric, which is cut on bias.

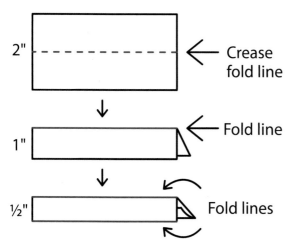

2" ← Crease fold line

1" ← Fold line

½" ← Fold lines

6. Use a bias-tape maker, if available, and follow the manufacturer's instructions. If no bias-tape maker is available, fold the fabric strip in half lengthwise and press. Open the strip, then fold the outside cut edges to the crease in the center of the fabric. Press these outside folds. Fold again to bring the outside folds together for the finished bias. Press folded edges.

HOW TO ATTACH DOUBLE-FOLDED BIAS TAPE

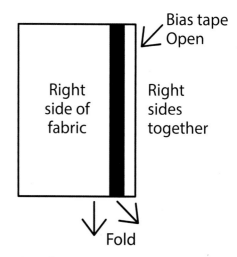

Bias tape Open

Right side of fabric

Right sides together

Fold

1. Line the raw edge of the bias tape with the raw edge of the quilted piece, right sides together, and pin or clip. Sew a straight stitch along inside crease.

2. Fold the bias tape up and over the edge of the quilt to the back of the project. The center fold of the bias tape will line up with the raw edge of the quilt. Press and pin or clip on the back.

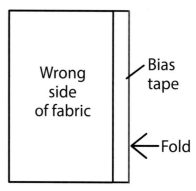

Wrong side of fabric

Bias tape

←Fold

3. Sew along the bias tape from the right side, close to the folded edge.

One-Inch Single-Fold Bias Tape

Only follow step 6 if making a single-fold bias tape. Do not fold a second time. This will not be cut on the bias, just folded like bias tape.

Stitch line to corner

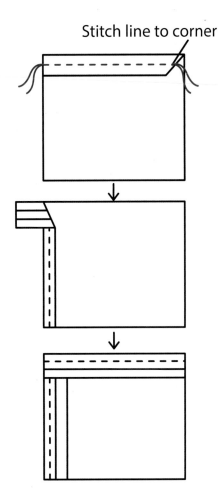

4. To complete the corners, stitch up to ¼" (6.4mm) from corner. Pivot and stitch diagonally to the corner. Fold the bias back along the diagonal stitch line. Bring the fold up to the batting edge. Stitch from the batting edge to the next corner.

Tip

When sewing an invisible zipper, I often use a fabric glue stick to hold each side in place as I sew it.

Pillow Finished with an Invisible Zipper

Use an invisible or standard zipper foot for this technique. Insert the zipper in the bottom seam of the pillow once the front and back are completed. Follow the zipper manufacturer's instructions for the application. Trim zipper ends as needed.

When the zipper is inserted, open the zipper. Matching right side and using a ¼" (6.4mm) seam allowance, sew the remaining pillow edges together. Trim corners as shown in step 1 of the Half-Inch Double-Fold Bias Tape (page 16). Turn the pillow right side out through the zipper opening, gently push out the corners, and insert the pillow form or stuffing.

ADDING A HIDDEN ZIPPER OPENING TO A PILLOW COVER

A hidden zipper is a lovely option for decorative pillow, especially if you have pets and might anticipate needing to clean the covers. It also makes it easy if you want to freshen up your look for the season: simply unzip, remove the insert from one cover, and use the insert for a different design. This technique can be used with or without applied trim.

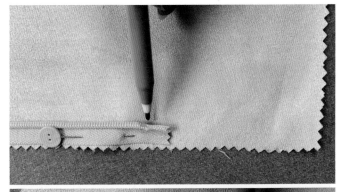

1. Unzip the zipper and flatten the tape with a warm iron. Place it face down on the right edge of the pillow front, so the left-side coils align with the seam allowance line. With a wash-away marker, mark in the seam allowance just above the zipper top stop and just above the zipper bottom stop. Pin to secure for stitching.

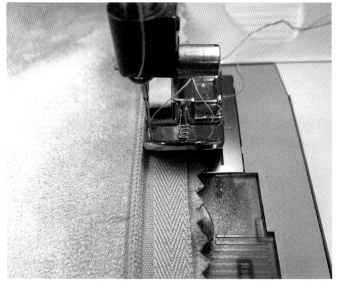

2. Using a zipper foot and right needle position, stitch from mark to mark, keeping close to the zipper coils.

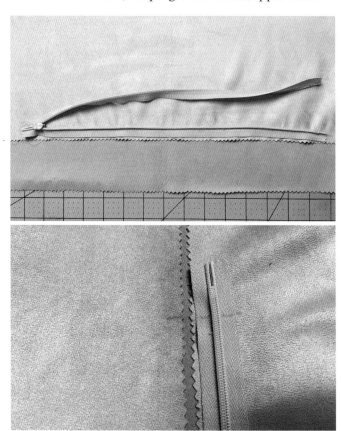

3. Zip up, and align the front prepared unit next to the back pillow unit. Using a water-soluble marking pen, mark across the zipper tape onto the corresponding back unit. This will make sure the front and back pieces match up once the zipper application is complete.

4. Unzip again, and press the remining side flat. Pin the unattached side of the zipper face down to the right side of the back pillow unit so the marks align. Stitch close to the zipper coils as in step 2, starting and stopping at the same points.

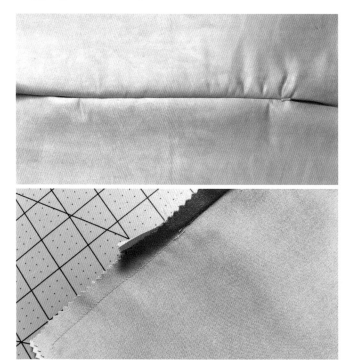

5. Zip up, so that the pillow front and back are right sides together. Stitch the pillow together at the top and bottom of the zipper, starting at ⅛" (3.2mm) outside the line of stitching that applied the zipper, and around the pillow. You want to stitch close to that previous stitch line but not so close you stitch through the zipper. Clip corners and push out with an awl or blunt-point instrument.

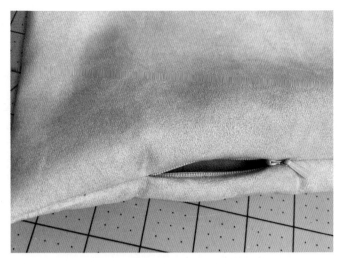

6. Turn the pillow right side out through the zipper opening. Stuff with a pillow form and zip closed.

PILLOW FINISHED WITHOUT A ZIPPER
Place the pillow back and front with right sides together. Using a ¼" (6.4mm) seam allowance, sew around the perimeter, leaving a 10" (25.4cm) opening for turning in the center of one edge. Trim corners.

Turn the pillow right side out, and gently push out the corners. Insert the pillow form and hand stitch the opening closed.

Shoulder Strap

1. Fold a long strip of strap fabric in half lengthwise and press.

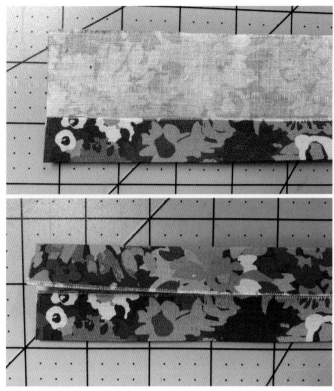

2. Open the fabric strip up. Fold the outside edges to the crease in the center of the strip. Press these outside folds.

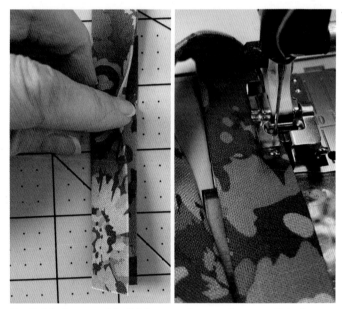

3. Fold the outside folds together and press. Stitch close to the edge on both long edges.

Folding ½" (1.3cm) strips is important for bias tape, binding, and shoulder straps.

Hem

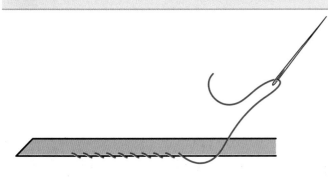

Whipstitch

Fold the edge to be hemmed under ¼" (6.4mm) and press. Topstitch close to the fold edge, or hand stitch with a whipstitch.

Gussets

1. Pinch together one bottom corner of the bag with seams flat. Make sure the seam is in the middle of the triangle on both sides. Place the acrylic ruler on the corner with a line following the seam. Measure 1½" (3.8cm) from tip of the point, and draw a line from one side to the other.

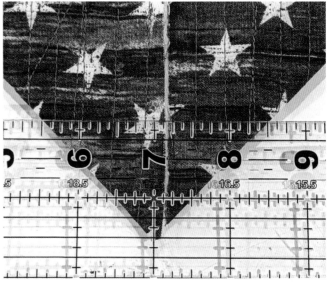

2. Sew across the line as shown, twice. Repeat on the other bottom corner. Cut away excess fabric leaving a ¼" (6.4mm) seam allowance. Flip the bag inside out.

Projects

The upcoming chapters demonstrate different Quilt As You Go block designs, joining techniques, and project ideas. I used a variety of common block designs, from log cabin to crazy quilt. These are all designed as beginner projects. Quilts will take longer than companion pieces, but it comes down to your creative desire.

All five joining techniques are used in the projects throughout this book. As I mentioned before, I recommend trying them all and then choosing the one that best fits your needs.

I intentionally incorporated plenty different fabrics and finishing techniques into these projects for additional interest. Be sure to refer back to those instructions if they are not laid out in the projects. Do not be afraid to put your own stamp of authenticity on your finished projects.

Scented Microwave Trivet

FINISHED SIZE: 8" x 8" (20.3 x 20.3cm)

Looking for a great gift for a bridal shower or thank you gift? This scented microwave trivet might just be the ticket. The pocket on the back is to hold a flat sachet of spice or potpourri. Heat the trivet in the microwave, and then insert the sachet into the pocket. The trivet can be heated in the microwave to keep food warm from the bottom of a casserole or pan as well as make the home smell as delicious as the meal. This trivet can be used as a coffee mug mat to keep coffee or tea warm. It is also cute under a small plant or vase of flowers.

This project uses Joining Technique 1 (page 12). Each block will be applied to the front of the batting only. The backing fabric will be added in a later step and then quilted with the stitch-in-the-ditch method.

FABRIC REQUIREMENTS

	Color	Yards	Inches	Centimeters
Fabric A	Dark Green Floral	⅙ yd	6"	15.2cm
Fabric B	Light Green Daisy	⅓ yd	12"	30.5cm
Fabric C	Yellow	⅙ yd	6"	15.2cm
Fabric D	Coral Dot	¼ yd	9"	22.9cm

SUPPLIES

- 8" x 8" (20.3 x 20.3cm) microwave batting
- Thread, matching Fabric B
- Quilt basting spray
- Needed tools (page 9)
- Fruit or spice flat sachet envelope

CUTTING INSTRUCTIONS

	Amount Needed	Use
Fabric A	(3) 1½" x 12" (3.8 x 30.5cm) strips	
Fabric B	(2) 1½" x 12" (3.8 x 30.5cm) strips	
	(1) 11" x 11" (27.9 x 27.9cm) square	bias tape
Fabric C	(2) 1½" x 12" (3.8 x 30.5cm) strips	
Fabric D	(2) 1½" x 12" (3.8 x 30.5cm) strips	
	(1) 8" x 8" (20.3 x 20.3cm) square	backing fabric
	(1) 5" x 8" (12.7 x 20.3cm) strip	pocket

INSTRUCTIONS

1. Mark the 8" x 8" (20.3 x 20.3cm) batting piece with a line diagonally from one corner to the other.

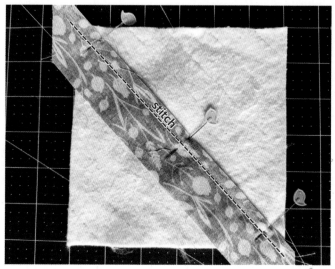

2. Place one of the Fabric C strips diagonally across the batting, wrong side down. Pin one Fabric A strip, right sides together, on top of the first strip. Stitch the two strips to the batting from the top-left to the bottom-right corner. **When stitched with ¼" (6.4mm) allowance, the seam should ride on the drawn diagonal line.**

A pocket is a great addition for any project, but you can make this without if you prefer.

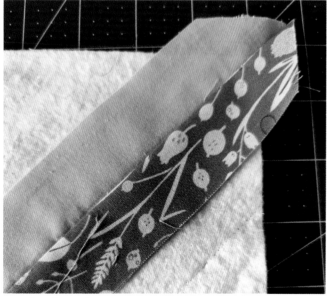

Fabric Placement

3. Flip the Fabric A strip open, away from the Fabric C strip. Iron the two strips flat on the batting.

4. Repeat steps 2–3 until all strips are attached, following the diagram. Square the block to 8" x 8" (20.3 x 20.3cm).

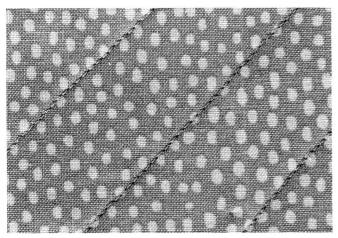

5. Spray the back of the batting with basting spray. Lay the backing fabric, wrong side down, on the batting. On the pieced front of the trivet, stitch-in-the-ditch through all three layers so the back of the trivet is quilted to match the piecing on the front.

ASSEMBLY & FINISHING

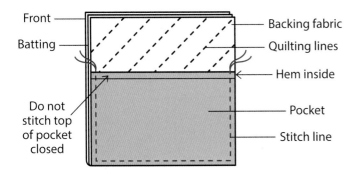

6. Hem one long side of the pocket fabric ¼" (6.4mm). Pin the pocket on the back of the trivet. Keep the hemmed edge open in the center of the trivet. The wrong side of the pocket will be against the trivet backing. Stitch the bottom and sides of the pocket to secure the trivet.

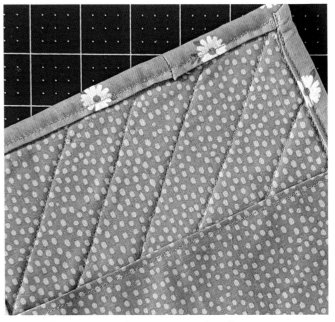

7. Use the 11" x 11" (27.9 x 27.9cm) Fabric B square to make ½" (1.3cm) double-fold bias tape. Attach the bias tape around the outside of the trivet.

8. Slip the sachet in the pocket or use without.

Microwave Bread Cover

A traditional bread cover keeps rolls or bread warm and fresh during meal preparation. It can be heated in the microwave to keep the bread warm throughout the meal. To use, place the warmed bread cover over your bread.

This project uses Joining Technique 1 (page 12). Each block will be applied to the front of the batting only. The backing fabric will be added in a later step and then quilted with the stitch-in-the-ditch method.

FABRIC REQUIREMENTS

		Color	Yards	Inches	Centimeters
Fabric A		Dark Green Floral	⅛ yd	6"	15.2cm
Fabric B		Light Green Daisy	½ yd	18"	45.7cm
Fabric C		Yellow	⅛ yd	6"	15.2cm
Fabric D		Coral Dot	⅛ yd	6"	15.2cm

SUPPLIES

- 18" x 18" (45.7 x 45.7cm) microwave batting
- Thread, matching Fabric B
- Quilt basting spray
- Needed tools (page 9)

CUTTING INSTRUCTIONS

	Amount Needed	Use
Fabric A	(12) 1½" x 12" (3.8 x 30.5cm) strips	
Fabric B	(8) 1½" x 12" (3.8 x 30.5cm) strips	
	(4) 8" x 8" (20.3 x 20.3cm) squares	backing fabric
	(1) 12" x 12" (30.5 x 30.5cm) square	bias tape
Fabric C	(8) 1½" x 12" (3.8 x 30.5cm) strips	
Fabric D	(8) 1½" x 12" (3.8 x 30.5cm) strips	
Batting	(4) 8" x 8" (20.3 x 20.3cm) squares	

Another way to use the bread cover is to put it in a basket first, then fold the corners over to keep the bread warm.

INSTRUCTIONS

Fabric Placement

1. Follow steps 1–4 of Microwave Scented Trivet (page 24) to make four blocks.

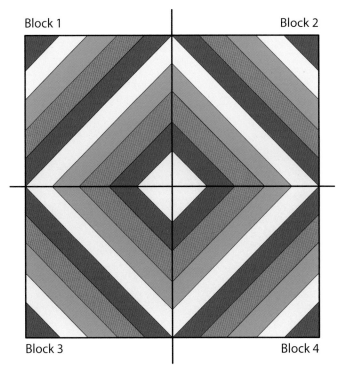

Block 1
Block 2
Block 3
Block 4

2. Using Technique 1 and referring to the diagram, sew the upper two blocks right sides together. Repeat for the bottom two blocks. Sew the top and bottom units together. Square the bread cover, and press all seams flat.

3. Spray the back of the batting with basting spray. Lay the backing fabric, wrong side down, on the batting. On the pieced front of the bread cover, stitch-in-the-ditch through all three layers so the back of the bread cover is quilted to match the piecing on the front.

FINISHING

4. Use the 12" x 12" (30.5 x 30.5cm) Fabric B square to make ½" (1.3cm) double-fold bias tape. Attach the bias tape around the outside of the bread cover.

Reversible Table Runner

FINISHED SIZE: 16" x 66" (40.6 x 167.6cm)

Are you looking for a bright, cheery table runner for your kitchen or dining room? This easy design is fun to create and use in your home. Even better—flip it over and use the reversed finished side for a fresh look.

This project uses Joining Technique 2 (page 13) to piece the block front, batting, and backing at the same time. The blocks will be attached with a narrow front strip and a wider back strip. Since you are quilting the block as you complete, there is no need for additional quilting. All seam allowances are ¼" (6.4mm) unless noted.

FABRIC REQUIREMENTS

	Color	Yards	Inches	Centimeters
Fabric A	Orange Print	3⅓ yds	120"	304.8cm
Fabric B	Green Floral	1 yd	36"	91.4cm
Fabric C	Orange Dot	½ yd	18"	45.7cm
Fabric D	Yellow Print	½ yd	18"	45.7cm

SUPPLIES

- 18" x 72" (45.7 x 182.9cm) needled cotton batting
- 2–3 spools light peach thread
- Quilt basting spray
- Needed tools (page 9)

The back of this table runner is just as nice as the front, which doubles your opportunities to use it.

CUTTING INSTRUCTIONS

	Amount Needed	Use
Fabric A	(24) 6" x 6" (15.2 x 15.2cm) squares	backing fabric
	(16) 2" x 10" (5.1 x 25.4cm) strips	
	(24) 3" x 6" (7.6 x 15.2cm) strips	backing fabric
	(36) 1" x 6½" (2.5 x 16.5cm) strips	narrow front strip
	(36) 2" x 6½" (5.1 x 16.5cm) strips	wide back strip
	(11) 1" x 18" (2.5 x 45.7cm) strips	narrow front strip
	(11) 2" x 18" (5.1 x 45.7cm) strips	wide back strip
	(1) 20" x 20" (50.8 x 50.8cm) square	bias tape
Fabric B	(16) 1¾" x 10" (4.4 x 25.4cm) strips	
	(16) 2½" x 6" (6.4 x 15.2cm) strips	
	(48) 2¼" x 2¼" (5.7 x 5.7cm) squares	
Fabric C	(8) 2¾" x 2¾" (7 x 7cm) squares; subcut on diagonal for 16 triangles	
	(8) 2½" x 6" (6.4 x 15.2cm) strips	
	(24) 2½" x 2½" (6.4 x 6.4cm) squares	
Fabric D	(8) 4½" x 4½" (11.4 x 11.4cm) squares; subcut on diagonal for 16 triangles	
	(16) 2½" x 2½" (6.4 x 6.4cm) squares	
Batting	(24) 6" x 6" (15.2 x 15.2cm) squares	
	(24) 3" x 6" (7.6 x 15.2cm) strips	

CENTER BLOCKS

1. Spray one side of the 6" x 6" (15.2 x 15.2cm) batting with basting spray. Lay the sticky side of the batting onto the wrong side of the 6" x 6" (15.2 x 15.2cm) Fabric A square.

2. Place a 2½" x 2½" (6.4 x 6.4cm) Fabric D square, wrong side to the batting, in the bottom-right corner. Match the sides.

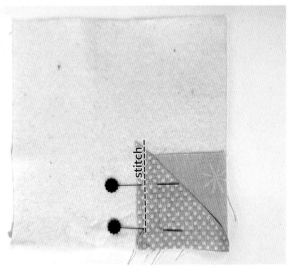

3. Place one Fabric C triangle on top of the Fabric D square, right sides together as shown. Stitch together, stopping ½" (1.3cm) from the outside edge. Iron seam open. **Note:** All stitching will be to ½" (1.3cm) from the outside batting edge.

4. Repeat step 3 with a second Fabric C triangle as shown. Iron seam open.

5. Stitch 1¾" x 10" (4.4 x 25.4cm) Fabric B strip to the Fabric C triangle edges with right sides together. Iron seam open.

6. Stitch 2" x 10" (5.1 x 25.4cm) Fabric A strip to the Fabric B strip with right sides together as shown. Iron seam open.

7. Stitch the long edge of a Fabric D triangle to the Fabric A strip. Iron seams open. This completes one Center block.

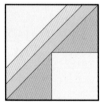

Make 16 Blocks

8. Repeat steps 2–8 for 15 more Center blocks. Square the blocks and set aside.

Tip

There will be 12 Side blocks on the right side of the table runner and 12 Side blocks on the left. Keep this in mind when stitching to leave ½" (1.3cm) unstitched on the outside edge.

END BLOCKS

9. Spray one side of the 6" x 6" (15.2 x 15.2cm) batting with basting spray. Lay the sticky side of the batting onto the wrong side of the 6" x 6" (15.2 x 15.2cm) Fabric A square.

10. Place a 2½" x 6" (6.4 x 15.2cm) Fabric B strip wrong side down, along one edge of the batting. Place a 2½" x 6" (6.4 x 15.2cm) Fabric C strip, right sides together, on top of the first strip. Stitch them together, leaving ½" (1.3cm) unstitched on the outside edge.

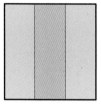

Make 8 Blocks

11. Flip the second strip back onto the batting and press the seam. Lay another 2½" x 6" (6.4 x 15.2cm) Fabric B strip on top of the last strip, right sides together. Flip the strip back and press the seam. This completes one End block. Make seven more. Square the blocks and set aside.

SIDE BLOCKS

12. Spray one side of the 3" x 6" (7.6 x 15.2cm) batting with basting spray. Lay the sticky side of the batting onto the wrong side of the 3" x 6" (7.6 x 15.2cm) Fabric A square.

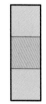

Make 24 Blocks

13. Lay one 2¼" x 2¼" (5.7 x 5.7cm) Fabric B square on a short end of the 3" x 6" (7.6 x 15.2cm) piece of batting. Place the 2½" x 2½" (6.4 x 6.4cm) Fabric C square on top of the first piece of fabric, right sides together. Stitch them together, leaving the ½" (1.3cm) unstitched outside edge. Flip the fabric back and press the seam.

14. Lay a second 2¼" x 2¼" (5.7 x 5.7cm) Fabric B square on top of the previous square, and stitch in place. Trim this strip to 3" x 6" (7.6 x 15.2cm). Make 23 more of these strip blocks.

ASSEMBLY & FINISHING

15. Lay out all blocks and strips as shown. Work in rows from one end of table runner to the other.

16. Use the 1" x 6½" (2.5 x 16.5cm) Fabric A strips and the 2" x 6½" (5.1 x 16.5cm) Fabric A strips to join the blocks: 1 Side block, 2 End blocks, and 1 Side block. Follow the instructions for Joining Technique 2. Use this technique to attach all blocks for the rows.

17. Using Technique 2, join the rows using 1" x 18" (2.5 x 45.7cm) Fabric A strips and 2" x 18" (5.1 x 45.7cm) Fabric A strips.

Tip

When joining, I stitched close to the edge but also did a random free-motion-quilting design of loops on the binding strips. This step can be handsewn as well.

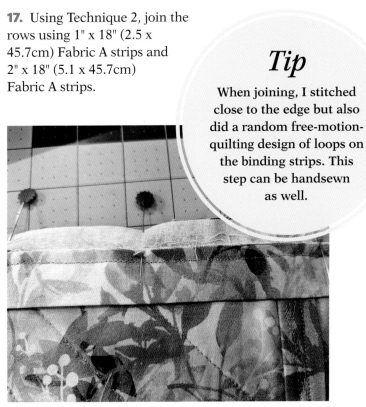

18. Use the 20" x 20" (50.8 x 50.8cm) Fabric A square to make bias tape for the perimeter. Attach the bias tape around the entire table runner.

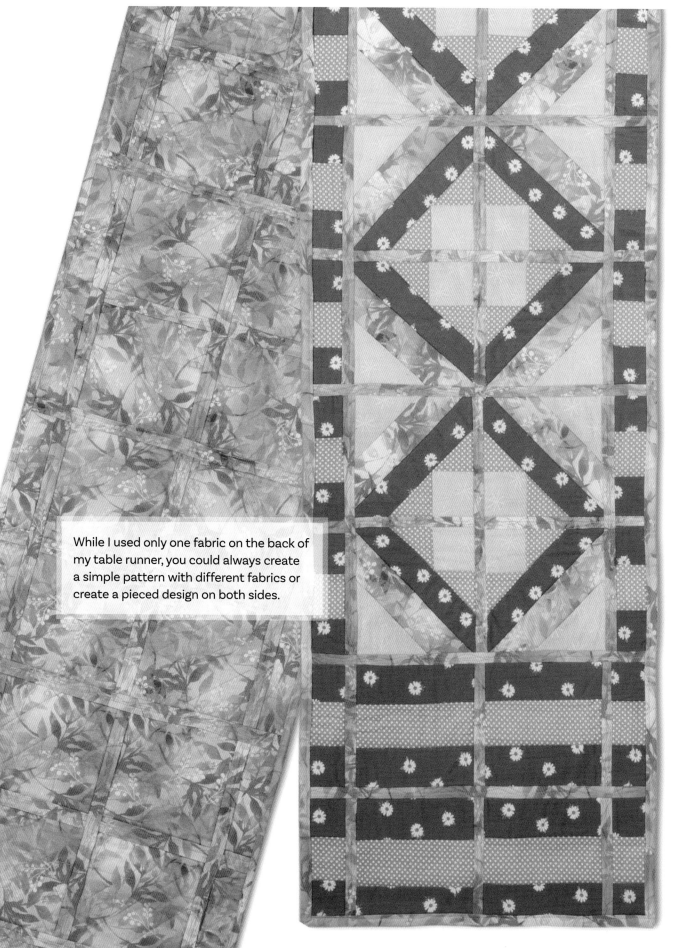

While I used only one fabric on the back of my table runner, you could always create a simple pattern with different fabrics or create a pieced design on both sides.

Silverware Pocket

This silverware pocket works nicely with the table runner in this chapter. Using the same fabrics, they'll coordinate and keep your table organized.

This project uses Joining Technique 2 (page 13) to piece the block front, batting, and backing at the same time. Since you are quilting the block as you complete, there is no need for additional quilting. All seam allowances are ¼" (6.4mm) unless noted.

FABRIC REQUIREMENTS (FOR EACH SILVERWARE POCKET)

	Color	Yards	Inches	Centimeters
Fabric A	Orange Print	⅓ yd	12"	30.5cm
Fabric B	Green Floral	¼ yd	9"	22.9cm
Fabric C	Orange Dot	¼ yd	9"	22.9cm
Fabric D	Yellow Print	¼ yd	9"	22.9cm

SUPPLIES
(FOR EACH SILVERWARE POCKET)

- 12" x 12" (30.5 x 30.5cm) needled cotton batting
- Light peach thread
- Quilt basting spray
- Needed tools (page 9)

CUTTING INSTRUCTIONS

	Amount Needed	Use
Fabric A	(1) 2¼" x 10½" (5.7 x 26.7cm) strip	
	(1) 4" x 10½" (10.2 x 26.7cm) strip	backing fabric
	(1) 10" x 10" (25.4 x 25.4cm) square	bias tape
	(1) 4" x 7" (10.2 x 17.8cm) strip	pocket backing fabric
	(1) 2¼" x 7½" (5.7 x 19.1cm) strip	pocket
Fabric B	(1) 2¼" x 2½" (5.7 x 6.4cm) rectangle	
	(1) 3½" x 2¼" (8.9 x 5.7cm) strip	pocket
Fabric C	(1) 2½" x 2½" (6.4 x 6.4cm) square	
	(1) 2¼" x 2¼" (5.7 x 5.7cm) square	pocket
Fabric D	(1) 2¼" x 1¾" (5.7 x 4.4cm) rectangle	pocket
	(1) 2¼" x 7¼" (5.7 x 18.4cm) strip	
Batting	(1) 4" x 10" (10.2 x 25.4cm) strip	
	(1) 4" x 7" (10.2 x 17.8cm) strip	pocket

BASE OF THE SILVERWARE POCKET

Back of the Base

1. Spray one side of the 4" x 10" (10.2 x 25.4cm) batting with basting spray. Lay the sticky side of the batting on the wrong side of the 4" x 10½" (10.2 x 26.7cm) Fabric A strip. Place vertically on the work surface.

2. Place the 2¼" x 7¼" (5.7 x 18.4cm) Fabric D strip, wrong side down, on the bottom-right corner of the batting.

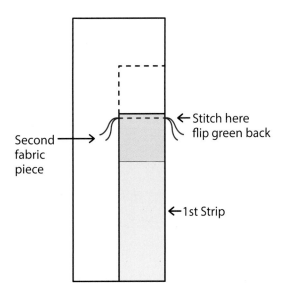

3. Place the 2¼" x 2½" (5.7 x 6.4cm) Fabric B rectangle, right sides together, at the top of the first fabric. Match the 2½" (6.4cm) side to the first piece of fabric. Stitch together. Flip the strip and press.

4. Place the 2½" x 2½" (6.4 x 6.4cm) Fabric C square on top of the last fabric piece, right sides together, and stitch. Flip the strip and press.

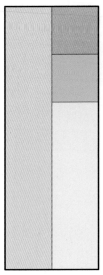

Base Front

5. Place the 2¼" x 10½" (5.7 x 26.7cm) Fabric A strip on top of the pieced unit, right sides together, and sew the seam. Flip the strip back and press the seam. Set aside.

POCKET OF THE SILVERWARE POCKET

6. Spray one side of the 4" x 7" (10.2 x 17.8cm) batting with basting spray. Lay the sticky side of the batting on the wrong side of the 4" x 7" (10.2 x 17.8cm) Fabric A strip. Place vertically on the work surface.

7. Place 2¼" x 2¼" (5.7 x 5.7cm) Fabric C square on the bottom-right corner of the batting.

8. Place 3½" x 2¼" (8.9 x 5.7cm) Fabric B strip, right sides together, at the top of the first fabric. Match the 2¼" (5.7cm) side to the first piece of fabric. Stitch along the upper edges. Flip the strip and press the seam.

9. Place the 2¼" x 1¾" (5.7 x 4.4cm) Fabric D rectangle on top of the Fabric C, right sides together, and stitch the upper edges.

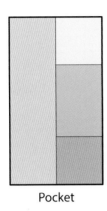

Pocket

10. Place the 2¼" x 7½" (5.7 x 19.1cm) Fabric A strip on top of the pieced right side of fabrics, right sides together, and sew a seam down the center of the piece. Flip the strip back and press the seams. Trim the batting to 4" x 7" (10.2 x 17.8cm).

ASSEMBLY & FINISHING

11. Use the 10" x 10" (25.4 x 25.4cm) Fabric A square to make bias tape for the perimeter. Stitch a 4" (10.2cm) bias strip along the top edge of the pocket unit.

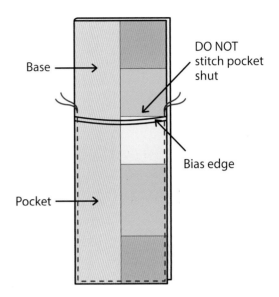

Base

DO NOT stitch pocket shut

Bias edge

Pocket

12. Lay the wrong side of the pocket to the right side of the Front block. Stitch the side seams and bottom seam, but leave the top open. Stitch bias tape all the way around the outside edge of the silverware pocket.

Scrappy Pillow

FINISHED SIZE: 16" x 16" (40.6 x 40.6cm)

This cozy quilted pillow is fun to make and easy to assemble. It's is a fantastic way to use up small pieces of fabric like crumb quilting. Remember, save your scraps, you may want them for future projects.

This project uses Joining Technique 3 (page 13) to piece the layers at the same time. The blocks will be attached with a wide front strip; because this is a pillow, we are not using the narrow strip on the back. Since you are quilting the block as you complete, there is no need for additional quilting. All seams will be ¼" (6.4mm) unless noted.

For this project, there is no backing fabric. If an inside lining of the pillow cover is desired, add the backing fabric to each side of the pillow before inserting the zipper. A zipper is optional; otherwise, the pillow form can be inserted and the case sewn shut.

FABRIC REQUIREMENTS

		Color	Yards	Inches	Centimeters
Fabric A		Floral Print	½ yd	18"	45.7cm
Fabric B		Black	¼ yd	9"	22.9cm
Fabric C		Teal		Remnants	
Fabric D		Purple		Remnants	
Fabric E		Gold		Remnants	
Fabric F		Green		Remnants	
Fabric G		Lavender		Remnants	

SUPPLIES

- 18" x 18" (45.7 x 45.7cm) needled cotton batting
- Lavender thread
- Invisible zipper (optional)
- 16" x 16" (40.6 x 40.6cm) pillow form
- Needed tools (page 9)

CUTTING INSTRUCTIONS

Note: The scrap widths are not an exact measurement but a general guide. If desired, you can also cut at an angle to achieve the wonky effect.

	Amount Needed	Use
Fabric A	(9) 3" x 6" (7.6 x 15.2cm) strips	
	(9) 2" x 6" (5.1 x 15.2cm) strips	wide front strip
	(2) 2" x 16" (5.1 x 40.6cm) strips	wide front strip
	(1) 3" x 16" (7.6 x 40.6cm) strip	
	(1) 10" x 16" (25.4 x 40.6cm) strip	
Fabric B	(2) 1" x 16" (2.5 x 40.6cm) strips	wide front strip
	(2) 30" x 2" (76.2 x 5.1cm) strips	bias tape
Fabric C	Several 4" x 1" (10.2 x 2.5cm) scraps	
Fabric D	Several 4" x 1" (10.2 x 2.5cm) scraps	
Fabric E	Several 4" x 1" (10.2 x 2.5cm) scraps	
Fabric F	Several 4" x 1" (10.2 x 2.5cm) scraps	
Fabric G	Several 4" x 1" (10.2 x 2.5cm) scraps	
Batting	(9) 6" x 6" (15.2 x 15.2cm) squares	
	(1) 16" x 16" (40.6 x 40.6cm) square	

FRONT OF THE PILLOW

1. Draw a line down the center the 6" x 6" (15.2 x 15.2cm) batting, creating two 3" (7.6cm) wide sides.

2. Place one of the scraps (C to G) wrong side to the batting, along the bottom edge. Keep to the left of the drawn line.

3. Place another scrap on top of the first. The second strip is attached at a slight angle to the first. Stitch a ¼" (6.4mm) seam along the top edge of the scraps. Flip the top scrap and press the seam flat. Stitch only from the center line of the batting to the outside edge of the batting. Sew to ½" (1.3cm) from the outside edges of the blocks throughout.

4. Repeat for the rest of this side of the batting square with random scraps. Trim the scraps along the center line and outside of the batting.

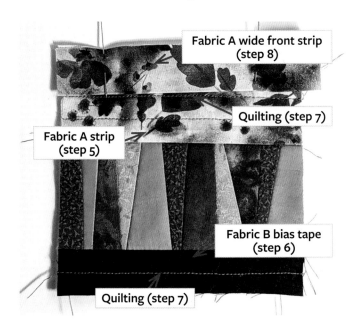

Fabric A wide front strip (step 8)

Quilting (step 7)

Fabric A strip (step 5)

Fabric B bias tape (step 6)

Quilting (step 7)

5. Place a 3" x 6" (7.6 x 15.2cm) Fabric A strip on top of the scrap unit, right sides together. Stitch together along the edge that's in the center of the block. Flip the A strip back and press the seam flat. Make eight more blocks. Square the blocks.

6. Use the 30" x 2" (76.2 x 5.1cm) Fabric B squares to make 60" (152.4cm) of bias tape (page 17). It should be 1" (2.5cm) wide. Stitch the bias tape to the scrap edge of the block. The raw edges of the bias tape should be flush with the block.

7. Quilt the Fabric A and B sides parallel to the seam, stitching straight lines that are ⅜" (1cm) apart. Repeat for the eight remaining blocks.

8. With the 2" x 6" (5.1 x 15.2cm) Fabric A strip, make a single-fold bias tape. It should be 1" (2.5cm) wide. Stitch the bias tape to the Fabric A side of the block. The raw edges should be flush with the edge of the block. Stitch along the outer edge. Trim the top and bottom of the new strip to the block. Flip this folded fabric strip to the outside of the batting and press the seam. Repeat for the eight remaining blocks.

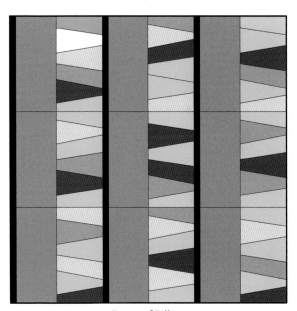

Front of Pillow

9. Lay out the nine blocks as shown. Take the first and second blocks of the first row and place the quilted sides together. Make sure the Fabric A folded strip is right sides together with the black edge of the next block. Stitch together and flip open. Join the second block to the third block the same way.

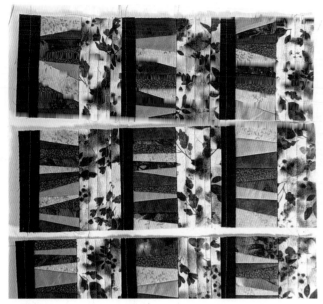

10. Repeat for two more rows of three blocks.

11. Fold a 2" x 16" (5.1 x 40.6cm) Fabric A strip in half (1" [2.5cm] wide). Attach to the first row, keeping the open edges along the outside of the block. Stitch in place. Flip the strip open and press the seam. With the same strip, attach the first row to the second row. Attach the third row in the same way. Square the completed pillow front and set aside.

BACK OF THE PILLOW

12. Draw a line 2" (5.1cm) in from one edge of the 16" x 16" (40.6 x 40.6cm) batting. Draw a second line 3" (7.6cm) from the first.

13. As in steps 2–4, make a 3" x 16" (7.6 x 40.6cm) strip of scraps sewn to the batting. Trim the overhanging scraps on both sides of the strip.

14. Stitch a 1" x 16" (2.5 x 40.6cm) Fabric B strip to each side of the scrap strip, right sides together. Flip these strips back and press the seams.

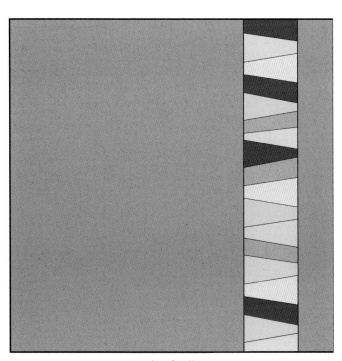

Back of Pillow

ASSEMBLY & FINISHING

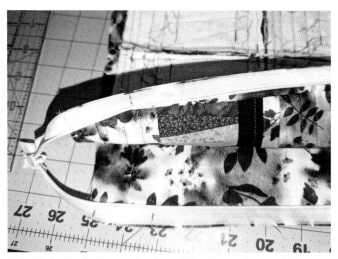

16. If desired, insert the invisible zipper (page 18).

17. Sew the front and back of the pillows together, right sides together. If using a zipper, leave the zipper open to pull the pillow through. If not, leave an 8" (20.3cm) opening when stitching the front and back together.

15. Stitch 10" x 16" (25.4 x 40.6cm) Fabric A strip to one black strip, right sides together. Stitch 3" x 16" (7.6 x 40.6cm) Fabric A strip to the other black strip, right sides together. Square the back of the pillow to the front.

18. Clip corners. Flip the pillow inside out, being sure to shape the corners; I use a dowel to push the shape gently. Carefully stuff the pillow form into the finished pillow cover, and work it around for an even fill. Zip the zipper shut or hand stitch the opening closed.

Each element adds a bit of texture and interest to this pillow, making this a stand-out piece of home decor.

Scrappy Journal Cover

FINISHED SIZE: 8½" x 10½" (21.6 x 26.7cm)

If you are like me, having a journal is a necessity. It could be a journal for quilting, daily events, or thoughts, but there is something comforting in writing everything on paper. This quilted journal cover is just the right size for a standard notebook. When the book is filled and finished, remove the journal, and slip another one in place.

This project uses Joining Technique 3 (page 13) to piece the layers at the same time. The blocks will be attached with a wide front strip; the backing fabric will be used instead of the narrow strip on the back. Since you are quilting the block as you complete, there is no need for additional quilting. All seams will be ¼" (6.4mm) unless noted.

FABRIC REQUIREMENTS

	Color	Yards	Inches	Centimeters
Fabric A	Floral Print	¼ yd	9"	22.9cm
Fabric B	Black		Remnants	
Fabric C	Teal	⅓ yd	12"	30.5cm
Fabric D	Purple	¼ yd	9"	22.9cm
Fabric E	Gold	⅓ yd	12"	30.5cm
Fabric F	Green		Remnants	
Fabric G	Lavender		Remnants	

SUPPLIES

- (2) 9" x 10½" (22.9 x 26.7cm) needled cotton batting
- Lavender thread
- Gold thread
- Quilt basting spray
- Needed tools (page 9)
- 7½" x 9¾" (19.1 x 24.8cm) notebook

CUTTING INSTRUCTIONS

Note: The scrap widths are not an exact measurement but a general guide. If desired, you can also cut at an angle to achieve the wonky effect.

	Amount Needed	Use
Fabric A	(1) 4" x 10½" (10.2 x 26.7cm) strip	
	(1) 2½" x 10½" (6.4 x 26.7cm) strip	
	(1) 9" x 10½" (22.9 x 26.7cm) strip	
Fabric B	(1) 2" x 10½" (5.1 x 26.7cm) strip	wide front strip
Fabric C	Several 3" x 1" (7.6 x 2.5cm) scraps	
	(1) 10½" x 17" (26.7 x 43.2cm) strip	backing fabric
Fabric D	Several 4" x 1" (10.2 x 2.5cm) scraps	
	(2) 3" x 10½" (7.6 x 26.7cm) strips	pocket
Fabric E	Several 4" x 1" (10.2 x 2.5cm) scraps	
	(1) 12" x 12" (30.5 x 30.5cm) square	bias tape
Fabric F	Several 4" x 1" (10.2 x 2.5cm) scraps	
Fabric G	Several 4" x 1" (10.2 x 2.5cm) scraps	

FRONT OF THE JOURNAL COVER

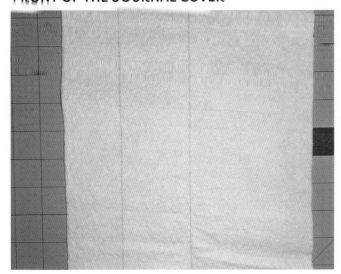

1. Draw a line 2" (5.1cm) away from one long edge of a batting piece. Draw a second line 4" (10.2cm) from the opposite side of the batting.

2. Place one of the scraps (C to G) wrong side to the batting, along the bottom edge. Keep between the drawn lines. Place another scrap on top of the first. Stitch a ¼" (6.4mm) seam along the top edge of the scraps. Flip the top scrap and press the seam flat. Stitch only from the center line of the batting to the outside edge of the batting. Sew to ½" (1.3cm) from the outside edges of the blocks throughout.

3. Repeat step 2 to fill the column of the batting square with random scraps. Finish with one 4" x 1" (10.2 x 2.5cm) scrap along the bottom edge. Trim the scraps along the two lines.

4. Place 2½" x 10½" (6.4 x 26.7cm) Fabric A strip, right sides together, on top of the scrap column. Align edges on the side near the narrower exposed batting and stitch together. Flip A back and press the seam flat.

5. Repeat with the 4" x 10½" (10.2 x 26.7cm) Fabric A strip, covering the other side of the block.

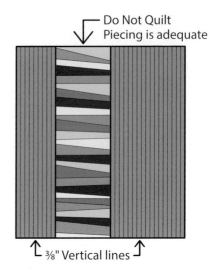

6. Quilt the Fabric A pieces parallel to the seam, stitching straight lines that are ⅜" (1cm) apart. Trim the front of the journal cover to 8½" x 10½" (21.6 x 26.7cm). Press all seams flat.

BACK OF THE JOURNAL COVER

Back of Journal Cover

7. Pin 9" x 10½" (22.9 x 26.7cm) Fabric A strip to the remaining batting piece. Quilt from top to bottom along the long side, stitching straight lines that are ⅜" (1cm) apart. Trim to 8½" x 10½" (21.6 x 26.7cm).

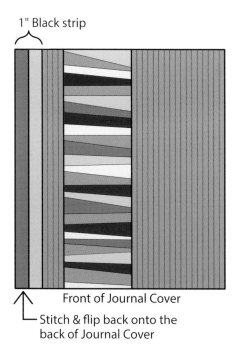

1" Black strip

Front of Journal Cover

Stitch & flip back onto the back of Journal Cover

8. Fold 2" x 10½" (5.1 x 26.7cm) Fabric B strip in half (1" [2.5cm] wide). Sew the folded strip to the front of the cover, right sides together, on the raw edge closest to the scrap column. Flip the strip back and press the seam.

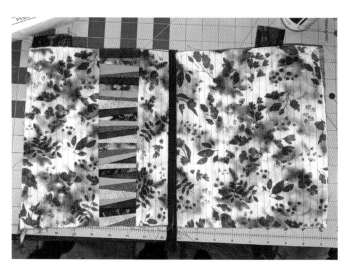

9. With the right sides together, sew the folded strip to the back of the journal cover. Press the seam flat. Trim any overhang.

ASSEMBLY & FINISHING

10. Place the 10½" x 17" (26.7 x 43.2cm) Fabric C piece, wrong sides together, on the inside of the journal cover. Stitch around the perimeter to hold in place. Stitch three lines down the center, through to the wide front strip.

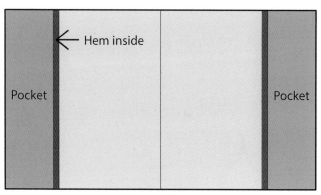

Hem inside

Pocket

Pocket

Journal Cover

11. Sew a ¼" (6.4mm) hem on one long edge of a 3" x 10½" (7.6 x 26.7cm) Fabric D strip. Join this strip to the left side of the inside cover, facing the hem toward the center of the cover. Repeat, joining the second strip to the right side.

12. Use the 12" x 12" (30.5 x 30.5cm) Fabric E square to make bias tape (page 16). Stitch the bias tape around the entire journal cover.

Flag Lap Quilt

FINISHED SIZE: 26" x 42" (66 x 106.7cm)

This lap quilt is perfect for snuggling under on a rainy or snowy day, but it is also fantastic as a picnic blanket. You could even hang it on the wall for a patriotic decoration.

This project uses Joining Technique 4 (page 14) to piece the block front, batting, and backing at the same time. The pieces will be assembled by stitching the blocks back-to-back. On the front, a binding will be added to cover the seams.

FABRIC REQUIREMENTS

	Color		Yards	Inches	Centimeters
Fabric A		Red Floral	¼ yd	9"	22.9cm
Fabric B		Red Dot	¼ yd	9"	22.9cm
Fabric C		Blue Star	½ yd	18"	45.7cm
Fabric D		Blue Stripe	¼ yd or 1 fat quarter	9"	22.9cm
Fabric E		Blue Floral	¼ yd or 1 fat quarter	9"	22.9cm
Fabric F		Blue Dot	¼ yd or 1 fat quarter	9"	22.9cm
Fabric G		Blue Solid	1⅓ yds	48"	121.9cm
Fabric H		Faded White Stripe	¼ yd or 1 fat quarter	9"	22.9cm
Fabric I		Off-White Floral	¼ yd or 1 fat quarter	9"	22.9cm
Fabric J		Faded White Star	¼ yd	9"	22.9cm
Fabric K		Tan	¼ yd or 1 fat quarter	9"	22.9cm

SUPPLIES

- 36" x 48" (91.4 x 121.9cm) needled cotton batting
- Navy blue thread
- Quilt basting spray
- Needed tools (page 9)

Tip

If you use a fabric with a definite direction to the print, you will want to be mindful of the placement of the fabric throughout this project.

CUTTING INSTRUCTIONS

	Amount Needed	Use
Fabric A	(10) 3" x 12" (7.6 x 30.5cm) strips	backing fabric
	Several small strips	
Fabric B	(8) 3" x 12" (7.6 x 30.5cm) strips	backing fabric
	Several small strips	
Fabric C	(18) 6" x 6" (15.2 x 15.2cm) squares	front & backing fabric
Fabric D	Several small strips	
Fabric E	Several small strips	
Fabric F	Several small strips	
Fabric G	(5) 2" x 16" (5.1 x 40.6cm) strips	binding
	(3) 2" x 22" (5.1 x 55.9cm) strips	binding
	(3) 2" x 28" (5.1 x 71.1cm) strips	binding
	(9) 2" x 42" (5.1 x 106.7cm) strips	binding
	(1) 18" x 18" (45.7 x 45.7cm) square	bias tape
Fabric H	(5) 3" x 12" (7.6 x 30.5cm) strips	backing fabric
	Several small strips	
Fabric I	(6) 3" x 12" (7.6 x 30.5cm) strips	backing fabric
	Several small strips	
Fabric J	(8) 3" x 12" (7.6 x 30.5cm) strips	backing fabric
	Several small strips	
Fabric K	(4) 3" x 12" (7.6 x 30.5cm) strips	backing fabric
	Several small strips	
Batting	(12) 6" x 6" (15.2 x 15.2cm) squares	
	(40) 3" x 12" (7.6 x 30.5cm) strips	

STAR BLOCKS

1. Spray one side of one 6" x 6" (15.2 x 15.2cm) batting with basting spray. Place sticky side down on the wrong side of a Fabric C square. Spray the other side of the batting, and place on the wrong side of another Fabric C square. Quilt vertical lines across the block ⅜" (1cm) apart.

2. Repeat for five more Star blocks. Square the blocks.

BLUE BLOCKS

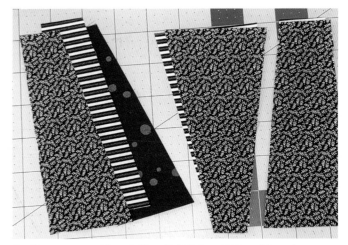

3. Spray one side of 6" x 6" (15.2 x 15.2cm) batting with basting spray. Place the sticky side down on the wrong side of Fabric C square. Flip the batting over, and place one strip (D to F) along one edge of the batting. The second strip is attached at a slight angle to the first. Stitch along the edge farthest from the starting side. Flip fabric and press seam flat. Repeat with more blue scraps to cover the batting. Ensure all pieces are attached on the sides, no open ends. Quilt vertical lines across the block ⅜" (1cm) apart.

4. Repeat for five more Blue blocks. Square the blocks.

RED STRIPE BLOCKS

5. Spray one side of one 3" x 12" (7.6 x 30.5cm) batting with basting spray. Place sticky side down on the wrong side of a 3" x 12" (7.6 x 30.5cm) Fabric A or B strip. Flip the batting over, and place one of the strips (A, B, or K) along one edge of the batting.

6. Place another red strip on top of the first, right sides together. The second strip of fabric should be attached at a slight angle to the first. Stitch along the edge farthest from the side of the block. Flip the fabric and press the seam flat.

7. Repeat with more red or tan scraps to cover the batting. Be sure all pieces are attached on all sides, no open ends. Quilt vertical lines across the block ⅜" (1cm) apart.

Random strips of different red fabrics and tan

8. Repeat steps 5–7 for 17 more Red Stripe blocks. Square the blocks.

9. Repeat steps 5–7 for four more Red Stripe blocks, using 3" x 12" (7.6 x 30.5cm) Fabric K strips as the backing fabric. Square the blocks.

WHITE STRIPE BLOCKS

10. Repeat steps 5–7 for 18 White Stripe blocks, using 3" x 12" (7.6 x 30.5cm) Fabric H, I, or J strips as the backing fabric. Then use white scraps for the front. Square the blocks.

ASSEMBLY

11. Lay out the Star blocks and Blue blocks, alternating them in the rows as shown. Stitch the first and second blocks of the first row, backing sides together. Follow step 3 for Joining Technique 4. Then join the third and fourth blocks in this row. Repeat for two more rows. Set them aside.

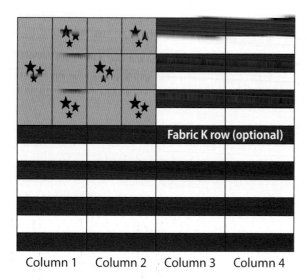

Column 1   Column 2   Column 3   Column 4

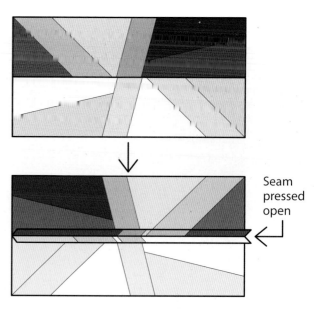

Seam
pressed
open

12. Lay out the Red Stripe blocks and White Stripe blocks as shown. If you are using Fabric K on the back of four blocks, those will be set in a row directly under the blue section.

13. Pick up the first and second blocks (red and white) in the third column. Place backing sides together, and stitch on the 12" (30.5cm) side. Repeat with the rest of the pairs in each column. Add the bottom row of blocks to the last red-and-white pair in each column.

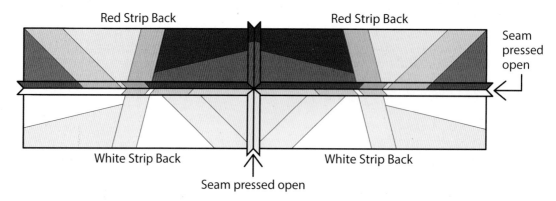

14. Stitch the top pair from Column 3 to the top pair in Column 4. Repeat with the remaining rows, including the bottom section with four blocks across.

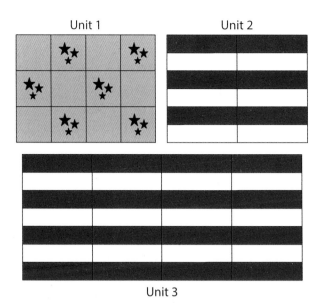

Unit 1   Unit 2

Unit 3

15. Stitch the rows of Stripe pairs together into two units, as shown. The tops of the third and fourth columns become Unit 2. The bottom rows become Unit 3. Join the rows of the blue section together to create Unit 1.

16. Stitch Unit 1 and Unit 2, backing sides together. Attach this unit to Unit 3, backing sides together. Open the flag quilt and iron all seams as flat as possible.

BINDING & FINISHING

17. Make 1" (2.5cm) bias tape using the 2" (5.1cm) wide Fabric G strips, following step 6 of the bias tape instructions (page 17). Iron-on adhesive can be used to hold the binding in place for stitching.

18. Place one 16" (40.6cm) bias tape between the first and second columns of Unit 1. Stitch the tape close to the edges. Repeat for the other two vertical stripes in Unit 1.

19. Use another 16" (40.6cm) bias tape to cover the vertical seam in Unit 2. Use 22" (55.9cm) bias tape to cover the vertical seams in Unit 3.

20. Use the 28" (71.1cm) bias tape to cover the horizontal seams in Unit 2. Alternate the rows, using only on the seams that do not extend into Unit 1. Place the final 16" (40.6cm) bias tape over the seam joining Unit 1 and 2.

21. Use 42" (106.7cm) bias tape to cover the rest of the horizontal seams, which extend across the whole quilt.

22. Use the 18" x 18" (45.7 x 45.7cm) Fabric G square to make ½" (1.3cm) double-fold bias tape. Attach the bias tape around the outside of the quilt.

Americana Tote Bag

This tote bag not only celebrates the United States, but it is also stylish and useful to carry the Flag Lap Quilt. There are so many wonderful red, white, and blue fabrics available; you should have no problem choosing the right fabrics for the job. Have fun with subtle prints.

This project uses Joining Technique 4 (page 14) to piece the block front, batting, and backing at the same time. The pieces will be assembled by stitching the blocks back-to-back. On the front, a binding will be added to cover the seams.

FABRIC REQUIREMENTS

	Color		Yards	Inches	Centimeters
Fabric A		Red Floral	¼ yd	9"	22.9cm
Fabric B		Red Dot	¼ yd	9"	22.9cm
Fabric C		Faded White Stripe	¼ yd	9"	22.9cm
Fabric D		Blue Solid	⅓ yd	12"	30.5cm
Fabric E		Blue Stripe	⅓ yd	12"	30.5cm
Fabric F		Blue Star	⅔ yd	24"	61cm

SUPPLIES

- 18" x 36" (45.7 x 91.4cm) needled cotton batting
- Thread of your choice
- Quilt basting spray
- 4 pairs of 1½" (3.8cm) plastic grommets
- Grommet template
- Pendant or bauble to attach to the strap
- Needed tools (page 9)

CUTTING INSTRUCTIONS

	Amount Needed	Use
Fabric A	(2) 5¼" x 14" (13.3 x 35.6cm) strips	
Fabric B	(2) 5¼" x 14" (13.3 x 35.6cm) strips	
Fabric C	(2) 5¼" x 14" (13.3 x 35.6cm) strips	
Fabric D	(2) 2½" x 36" (6.4 x 91.4cm) strips	shoulder strap
Fabric E	(1) 10" x 10" (25.4 x 25.4cm) square	bias tape
Fabric F	(2) 15" x 15" (38.1 x 38.1cm) squares	lining
	(2) 4" x 15" (10.2 x 38.1cm) strips	
	(2) 2" x 36" (5.1 x 91.4cm) strips	shoulder strap
	(1) 1" x 9" (2.5 x 22.9cm) strip	pendant loop
Batting	(2) 15" x 15" (38.1 x 38.1cm) squares	

INSTRUCTIONS

1. Spray one side of the 15" x 15" (38.1 x 38.1cm) batting with basting spray. Lay the sticky side of the batting onto the wrong side of the 15" x 15" (38.1 x 38.1cm) Fabric F square. Flip the batting over.

2. Place one Fabric A strip in one corner of the batting front, wrong side to the batting. Place one Fabric C strip on top of Fabric A, right sides together. Sew through the batting and backing fabric on the side away from the batting edge.

3. Repeat with one Fabric B strip on Fabric C, sewing on the side next to the exposed batting. Quilt the strips of fabric from top to bottom, vertically, in lines ⅜" (1cm) apart.

4. Place one 4" x 15" (10.2 x 38.1cm) Fabric F strip on top of the three pieces, right sides together, perpendicular to the strips. Stitch on the bottom edge of the other fabrics, at the end near the batting. Quilt the Fabric F strip horizontally, in lines ⅜" (1cm) apart.

5. Repeat steps 1–4 to complete the back of the bag.

6. Place the front and back of the bag right sides together. The horizontal strip of Fabric F will be at the bottom of the bag on both sides. Stitch the sides and the bottom of the bag, leaving the top open. Stitch 1½" (3.8cm) gussets in the bottom of the bag (page 21).

7. Draw a circle, using the template that comes with the grommets, on the top of each red fabric stripe. Refer to the photo on page 59 for positioning. Cut the grommet hole open, and insert the grommet back from behind. Secure by pressing the grommet front onto the back piece with force through the hole. Repeat for the three remaining grommets, making sure to align evening side to side and back to front.

8. Use the 10" x 10" (25.4 x 25.4cm) Fabric E square to make ½" (1.3cm) double-fold bias tape (page 16). Attach the bias tape around the top edge of the bag.

9. Use the 2½" x 36" (6.4 x 91.4cm) Fabric D strip to make a shoulder strap. Fold in both long edges on your D strip by ½" (1.3cm) and press. Set aside. Repeat using your 2" x 36" (5.1 x 91.4cm) Fabric F strip.

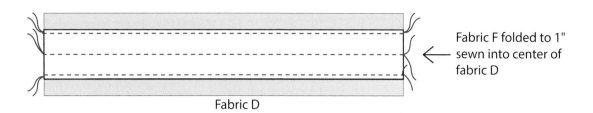

Fabric F folded to 1" ← sewn into center of fabric D

Fabric D

10. Position the Fabric F strip, folded side down, in the center of the Fabric D strip, folded side up. Glue baste if desired or pin. Edge stitch down each long side of Fabric F strip to attach. Add a third line of stitching down the center. Repeat for a second strap.

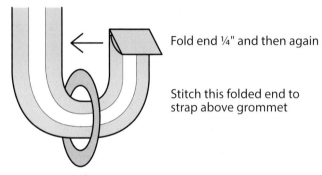

Fold end ¼" and then again

Stitch this folded end to strap above grommet

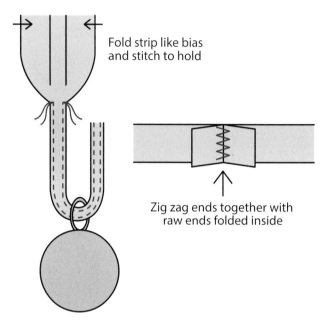

Fold strip like bias and stitch to hold

Zig zag ends together with raw ends folded inside

11. Insert one end of a strap into one grommet hole from the front of the bag. Fold that end over by ½" (1.3cm) twice, enclosing the raw edge. Stitch this folded end of the handle close to the top of the bag. Be careful not to catch the top of the bag in your stitch line. Repeat for three other handle ends.

12. Fold 1" x 9" (2.5 x 22.9cm) Fabric F strip in half (¼" [6.4mm] wide) as shown for strap construction. Stitch close to long open edge to secure. Slip the pendant onto this strip, wrap around the front handle, and sew the ends together, hiding the raw edges inside a fold.

Adding a medallion to this bag makes your handmade project look professional and unique.

Modern Log Cabin Pillow

FINISHED SIZE: 16" x 16" (40.6 x 40.6cm)

A beautiful log cabin design on the front and a four-stripe design on the back is elevated by the fabulous chosen fabric. Colorful, comfortable décor that is completed in an afternoon. The invisible zipper finishes the simple design that can be laundered as needed.

This project uses Joining Technique 5 (page 15) to piece the layers at the same time. Join the blocks, backing to backing, close to the blocks; then fold the excess fabric around to frame the blocks. This pillow has a backing fabric to all the blocks. I sometimes like to use a finished backing as a lining, so the pillow form slides in and out easily without snagging into an unfavorable twisted position.

FABRIC REQUIREMENTS

	Color		Yards	Inches	Centimeters
Fabric A		Light Blue Floral	⅓ yd	12"	30.5cm
Fabric B		Dark Blue Small Floral	⅔ yd	24"	61cm
Fabric C		Mauve Dot	¼ yd	9"	22.9cm
Fabric D		Dark Blue Large Floral	¼ yd	9"	22.9cm

SUPPLIES

- 36" x 36" (91.4 x 91.4cm) needled cotton batting
- 20" (50.8cm) invisible zipper in black or navy
- Dark blue thread
- Quilt basting spray
- 16" x 16" (40.6 x 40.6cm) pillow form
- Needed tools (page 9)

CUTTING INSTRUCTIONS

	Amount Needed	Use
Fabric A	(4) 2½" x 2½" (6.4 x 6.4cm) squares	front
	(4) 2½" x 7½" (6.4 x 19.1cm) strips	front
	(4) 2½" x 9" (6.4 x 22.9cm) strips	back
Fabric B	(4) 2½" x 2½" (6.4 x 6.4cm) squares	front
	(4) 2½" x 9" (6.4 x 22.9cm) strips	back
	(4) 11" x 11" (27.9 x 27.9cm) squares	front backing fabric
	(4) 11" x 11" (27.9 x 27.9cm) squares	back backing fabric
Fabric C	(4) 2½" x 5" (6.4 x 12.7cm) strips	front
	(4) 2½" x 7½" (6.4 x 19.1cm) strips	front
	(4) 2½" x 9" (6.4 x 22.9cm) strips	back
Fabric D	(4) 2½" x 5" (6.4 x 12.7cm) strips	front
	(4) 2½" x 9" (6.4 x 22.9cm) strips	front
	(4) 2½" x 9" (6.4 x 22.9cm) strips	back
Batting	(4) 9" x 9" (22.9 x 22.9cm) squares	front
	(4) 9" x 9" (22.9 x 22.9cm) squares	back

FRONT OF THE PILLOW

1. Spray one side of the 9" x 9" (22.9 x 22.9cm) batting with basting spray. Lay the sticky side of the batting onto the wrong side of the 11" x 11" (27.9 x 27.9cm) Fabric B square.

2. Place 2½" x 2½" (6.4 x 6.4cm) Fabric A square in the bottom-right corner of the batting, right side up. Place 2½" x 2½" (6.4 x 6.4cm) Fabric B square on top of the first square, right sides together. Stitch a ¼" (6.4mm) seam on the left side, away from the closest batting edge. Press the seam.

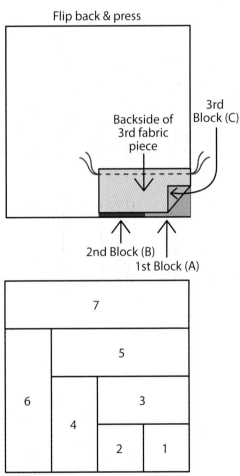

Block order to stitch like above

3. Stitch 2½" x 5" (6.4 x 12.7cm) Fabric C strip on top of the first two pieces of fabric, right sides together. Flip the fabric and press the seam. Stitch 2½" x 5" (6.4 x 12.7cm) Fabric D strip, right sides together, on top of the left side of the unit. Flip the fabric and press the seam.

4. Stitch 2½" x 7½" (6.4 x 19.1cm) Fabric A strip on top of the unit, right sides together. Flip the fabric and press the seam. Stitch 2½" x 7½" (6.4 x 19.1cm) Fabric C strip, right sides together, on top of the left side of the unit. Flip the fabric, and press the seam.

5. Stitch 2½" x 9" (6.4 x 22.9cm) Fabric D strip on top of the unit, right sides together. Flip the fabric and press the seam. Trim the pieced front fabrics to the batting. **Do not cut the backing fabric or batting.**

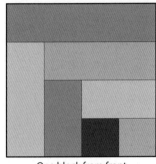

One block from front

6. Repeat steps 1–5 to make three more Log Cabin blocks for the pillow front.

7. Join two blocks together using Joining Technique 5. Make sure the design of the Log Cabin is in the direction you desire when sewing them together.

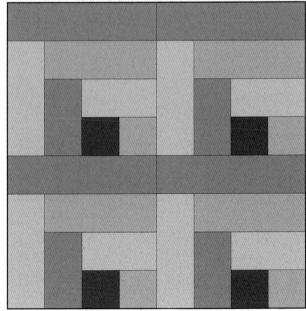

Front of Pillow

8. Repeat with the other two blocks. Join the two units together, but do not stitch the outside edges of the pillow front until later, when the pillow is assembled.

BACK OF THE PILLOW

9. Spray one side of the 9" x 9" (22.9 x 22.9cm) batting with basting spray. Lay the sticky side of the batting onto the wrong side of the 11" x 11" (27.9 x 27.9cm) Fabric B square.

10. Place 2½" x 9" (6.4 x 22.9cm) Fabric A strip along one edge. Stitch 2½" x 9" (6.4 x 22.9cm) Fabric D strip on top, right sides together. Flip the fabric and press the seam. Stitch 2½" x 9" (6.4 x 22.9cm) Fabric C strip on top of Fabric D, right sides together. Flip the fabric and press the seam.

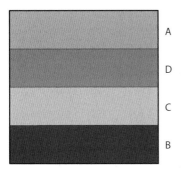

11. Stitch 2½" x 9" (6.4 x 22.9cm) Fabric D strip on top of Fabric C, right sides together. Flip the fabric and press the seam. Trim the pieced front fabrics to the batting. **Do not cut the backing fabric or batting.**

12. Quilt this block with a vertical line every ⅜" (1cm) from one side to the other.

13. Repeat steps 9–12 to make three more Four Stripe blocks for the pillow back.

14. Join two blocks together using Joining Technique 5. Make sure the design of the Log Cabin is in the direction you desire when sewing them together.

15. Repeat with the other two blocks. Join the two units together, but do not stitch the outside edges of the pillow back.

ASSEMBLY & FINISHING

16. Insert the invisible zipper (page 18) and finish the pillow. Insert the pillow form.

17. If no zipper is being used, place the front and back of the pillow, right sides together. Stitch all around the outside edges, leaving 9" (22.9cm) open on one side. Stitch close to the batting. Open the block backing, and fold the raw edge under twice, so the raw edge is hidden inside like bias. Stitch along the folded edge. Hand stitch the opening shut after the pillow is inserted.

Log Cabin Tablet Tote Bag

This beautiful tote bag has a log cabin front and striped back, making it a fashionable accessory to carry your electronic tablet, pens, notebook, or whatever you need. The strap is designed as a crossbody strap for hands-free travel.

This project uses Joining Technique 5 (page 15) to piece the layers at the same time. Join the blocks, backing to backing, close to the blocks; then fold the excess fabric around to frame the blocks.

FABRIC REQUIREMENTS

	Color		Yards	Inches	Centimeters
Fabric A		Light Blue Floral	⅓ yd	12"	30.5cm
Fabric B		Dark Blue Small Floral	¼ yd	9"	22.9cm
Fabric C		Mauve Dot	⅔ yd	24"	61cm
Fabric D		Dark Blue Large Floral	⅓ yd	12"	30.5cm

SUPPLIES

- 24" x 24" (61 x 61cm) needled cotton batting
- Dark blue thread
- 4 silver metal rings, 1" (2.5cm) wide
- 2 silver clasps, with 1" (2.5cm) metal D ring on opposite end
- Quilt basting spray
- Needed tools (page 9)

CUTTING INSTRUCTIONS

	Amount Needed	Use
Fabric A	(1) 2" x 4½" (5.1 x 11.4cm) strip	front
	(1) 2" x 6" (5.1 x 15.2cm) strip	front
	(1) 2" x 9½" (5.1 x 24.1cm) strip	front
	(1) 2" x 9" (5.1 x 22.9cm) strip	back
	(1) 2" x 4" (5.1 x 10.2cm) strip	flap
Fabric B	(1) 2" x 5" (5.1 x 12.7cm) strip	front
	(1) 2" x 6" (5.1 x 15.2cm) strip	front
	(1) 2½" x 9" (6.4 x 22.9cm) strip	back
	(2) 2" x 4" (5.1 x 10.2cm) strips	flap
Fabric C	(1) 2½" x 3½" (6.4 x 8.9cm) strip	front
	(1) 2" x 7½" (5.1 x 19.1cm) strip	front
	(1) 2" x 9" (5.1 x 22.9cm) strip	front
	(1) 2½" x 9" (6.4 x 22.9cm) strip	back
	(1) 2" x 4" (5.1 x 10.2cm) strip	flap
	(2) 11" x 14" (27.9 x 35.6cm) strips	backing fabric
	(1) 4" x 9" (10.2 x 22.9cm) strip	backing fabric
Fabric D	(1) 2½" x 3½" (6.4 x 8.9cm) strip	front
	(1) 2" x 7½" (5.1 x 19.1cm) strip	front
	(1) 2" x 9" (5.1 x 22.9cm) strip	front
	(2) 2½" x 9" (6.4 x 22.9cm) strips	back
	(2) 2" x 4" (5.1 x 10.2cm) strips	flap
	(1) 4" x 44" (10.2 x 111.8cm) strip	shoulder strap
	(2) 4" x 12" (10.2 x 30.5cm) strips	bag strap
	(1) 2" x 10" (5.1 x 25.4cm) strip	ring attachment
Batting	(1) 9" x 12" (22.9 x 30.5cm) strip	front
	(1) 9" x 12" (22.9 x 30.5cm) strip	back
	(1) 4" x 9" (10.2 x 22.9cm) strip	flap

FRONT OF THE BAG

1. Spray one side of the 9" x 12" (22.9 x 30.5cm) batting with basting spray. Lay the sticky side of the batting onto the wrong side of the 11" x 14" (27.9 x 35.6cm) Fabric C strip.

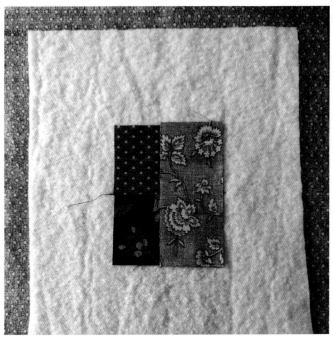

2. Place 2½" x 3½" (6.4 x 8.9cm) Fabric D strip in the center of the block. Stitch 2½" x 3½" (6.4 x 8.9cm) Fabric C strip on top, right sides together, sewing on the bottom edge. Flip the fabric and press the seam. Stitch 2" x 4½" (5.1 x 11.4cm) Fabric A strip, right sides together, on top of the left side of the first two pieces. Flip the fabric and press the seam.

3. Stitch 2" x 5" (5.1 x 12.7cm) Fabric B strip on the top, right sides together. Flip and press. Stitch 2" x 6" (5.1 x 15.2cm) Fabric A strip down the right side of the unit, right sides together. Flip and press. Stitch 2" x 6" (5.1 x 15.2cm) Fabric B strip along the bottom, right sides together. Flip and press.

4. Stitch 2" x 7½" (5.1 x 19.1cm) Fabric D strip along the left side of the unit, right sides together. Flip and press. Stitch 2" x 7½" (5.1 x 19.1cm) Fabric C strip on the top, right sides together. Flip and press. Stitch 2" x 9" (5.1 x 22.9cm) Fabric D strip along the right side of the unit, right sides together. Flip and press.

Front of Bag

5. Stitch 2" x 9" (5.1 x 22.9cm) Fabric C strip across the bottom of the unit, right sides together. Flip and press. Place 2" x 9½" (5.1 x 24.1cm) Fabric A strip along the top of the unit, right sides together. Flip and press.

6. Quilt the front as desired. Trim the pieced front fabrics to the batting. **Do not cut the backing fabric or batting.** You may want to pin back the backing fabric to trim with a rotary cutter.

BACK OF THE BAG

7. Spray one side of the 9" x 12" (22.9 x 30.5cm) batting with basting spray. Lay the sticky side of the batting onto the wrong side of the 11" x 14" (27.9 x 35.6cm) Fabric C strip.

8. Place 2½" x 9" (6.4 x 22.9cm) Fabric D strip along one short edge. Stitch 2½" x 9" (6.4 x 22.9cm) Fabric C strip on top of the previous strip, right sides together. Flip the fabric and press the seam.

Back of Bag

9. Stitch 2½" x 9" (6.4 x 22.9cm) Fabric B strip on top, right sides together. Flip and press. Stitch 2½" x 9" (6.4 x 22.9cm) Fabric D strip on top, right sides together. Flip and press. Stitch 2½" x 9" (6.4 x 22.9cm) Fabric A strip on top, right sides together. Flip and press.

10. Quilt this block with a vertical line every ⅜" (1cm) from the top to the bottom. Trim the pieced front fabrics to the batting. **Do not cut the backing fabric or batting.**

FLAP OF THE BAG

11. Spray one side of the 4" x 9" (10.2 x 22.9cm) batting with basting spray. Lay the sticky side of the batting onto the wrong side of the 4" x 9" (10.2 x 22.9cm) Fabric C strip.

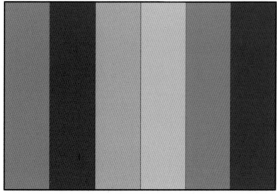

Flap of Bag

12. Stitch 2" x 4" (5.1 x 10.2cm) strips to the batting, in this order: D, B, A, C, D, B. Use steps 8 and 9 for reference.

13. Quilt this block with a vertical line every ⅜" (1cm) from the top to the bottom. Note that these lines are horizontal when the flap is attached to the bag. Trim the pieced front fabrics to the batting. **Do not cut the backing fabric or batting.**

ASSEMBLY & FINISHING

14. Using Joining Technique 5, stitch the flap and the back of the bag together. For the back of the bag, only fold the backing fabric where the two pieces join. For the flap, once joined, all sides of the backing fabric can be folded like bias tape. Miter the binding at the corners.

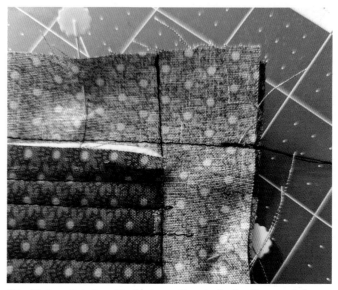

15. Using Joining Technique 5, stitch the front of the bag and the back of the bag together. All sides of the backing fabric can now be folded like bias tape.

16. Use the 4" x 44" (10.2 x 111.8cm) Fabric D strip to make a 1" (2.5cm) wide shoulder strap. Slip the two silver metal clasps onto the strap. Fold the ends over by ¾" (1.9cm) twice, and stitch the end to the strap, ensuring the metal finding is nestled inside the loop. Repeat for the other end of the shoulder strap.

17. To create a foundation for the attachment rings, fold the 2" x 10" (5.1 x 25.4cm) Fabric D strip in half lengthwise, wrong sides together. Open, then press each long raw edge toward the center so they meet at the created centerfold. Press flat. Slip one silver ring onto one end of the created strip. Fold the short raw end over ¾" (1.9cm) twice and pin. Repeat on the opposite side of the strip with the second ring.

18. Lay the flap open. Stitch the Fabric D strip with rings on either end to the inside seam, where the flap and back of the bag join.

19. Use the 4" x 12" (10.2 x 30.5cm) Fabric D straps to create the decorative straps extending from the flap as shown. Fold as you did for the shoulder straps and stitch down the long open end.

20. Hand stitch the metal rings to the flap, 1" (2.5cm) from the top of the bag. Ensure equal spacing on each side.

The faux "bias trim" here is actually the lining fabric folded over the flap edge twice and stitched in place.

Flannel Baby Quilt

FINISHED SIZE: 30" x 36" (76.2 x 91.4cm)

This baby quilt pattern is easy to follow and makes a great shower gift for that special little one. Choose a fun main print and then accent it with three coordinating prints. QAYG with flannel is the same as with cotton but even cozier when finished.

This project uses Joining Technique 5 (page 15) to piece the layers at the same time. Join the blocks, backing to backing, close to the blocks; then fold the excess fabric around to frame the blocks.

FABRIC REQUIREMENTS

	Color		Yards	Inches	Centimeters
Fabric A		Alphabet Print	2 yds	72"	182.9cm
Fabric B		Pink Print	¼ yd	9"	22.9cm
Fabric C		Yellow Dot	¼ yd	9"	22.9cm
Fabric D		Mint Print	¼ yd	9"	22.9cm

SUPPLIES

- 30" x 36" (76.2 x 91.4cm) needled cotton batting
- 2 spools light pink thread
- 4 yards (3.7m) pink floral lace trim
- Needed tools (page 9)

CUTTING INSTRUCTIONS

	Amount Needed	Use
Fabric A	(30) 8" x 8" (20.3 x 20.3cm) squares	backing fabric
	(15) 6" x 6" (15.2 x 15.2cm) squares	
Fabric B	(15) 2¼" x 6" (5.7 x 15.2cm) strips	
Fabric C	(15) 2½" x 6" (6.4 x 15.2cm) strips	
Fabric D	(15) 2¼" x 6" (5.7 x 15.2cm) strips	
Batting	(30) 6" x 6" (15.2 x 15.2cm) squares	

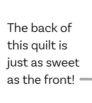

The back of this quilt is just as sweet as the front! →

STRIP BLOCKS

1. Center 6" x 6" (15.2 x 15.2cm) batting on the wrong side of 8" x 8" (20.3 x 20.3cm) Fabric A square. Pin the batting on each side to keep the batting and fabric together as you piece the front.

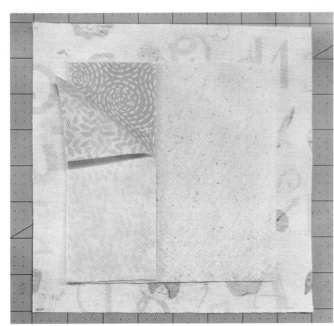

2. Pin a Fabric B strip, right side up, to the top of the batting, lining up the left edges. Stitch a Fabric C strip on top of the first strip, right sides together. Flip the fabric and press the seam.

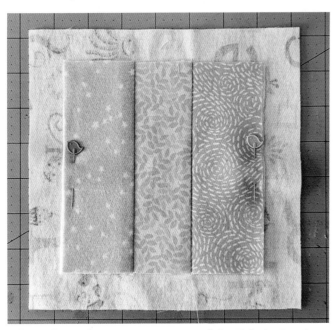

3. Stitch a Fabric D strip on top of the Fabric C strip, right sides together. Flip the fabric and press the seam. Pin the strips on the outside edges to the batting and backing for quilting.

4. Quilt the Fabric B and D strips with lines parallel to the seam, continuing ⅜" (1cm) apart. Do not quilt the center strip.

5. Repeat steps 1–4 to make 14 more Stripe blocks.

SOLID BLOCK

6. Center 6" x 6" (15.2 x 15.2cm) batting on the wrong side of 8" x 8" (20.3 x 20.3cm) Fabric A square. Pin 6" x 6" (15.2 x 15.2cm) Fabric A square to the batting, wrong side down. Line up the corners.

7. Starting at the bottom-left side, with design front and back upright, quilt vertical lines every ⅜" (1cm).

8. Repeat steps 6 and 7 to make 14 more Solid blocks.

Tip

As you piece and quilt these blocks, be conscious of the direction of the main print fabric. If it has a vertical design, for example, then it should be placed in the quilt upright. The back pieces should all be upright.

ASSEMBLY & FINISHING

30 blocks - each 6″ x 6″

9. Lay the blocks out according to the diagram. Pay attention to the orientation of the Stripe blocks.

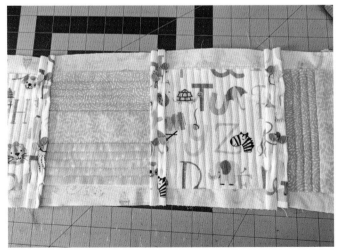

10. Stitch the first block to the second block in the first row, referring to step 3 of Joining Technique 5. Repeat with the rest of the blocks in the first row.

11. Continue with the remainder of Technique 5 on the first row. Fold the raw edges so they are hidden inside like bias tape. Stitch along the fold. Do not fold the ends of each row, which will be done when all rows are joined.

12. Repeat steps 10 and 11 for the remaining rows.

13. Stitch the first and second row together as in step 11, making sure to match all seams and fabric edges. Repeat for the remaining rows until they are all connected.

Zigzag any edges that are not joined between the blocks.

14. Stitch the floral lace trim down the seams between the columns.

15. Where the block "edgings" meet around quilt lining, zigzag them together. Stitch the backing fabric on the outside of the quilt, folding to the right side of the quilt twice and edge stitching as in Technique 5.

Flannel Tag Toy

Babies love tag toys because of the different textures, toys or pacifiers attached, and the crinkling noise from within. Did you know you could QAYG a tag toy? This fun, soft, and crinkly toy will be a hit for an incredibly special child.

This project uses Joining Technique 1 (page 12). Each block will be applied to the front of the batting only. However, we won't be stitching-in-the-ditch. The backing fabric will be added separately when the front is completed—tags, toys, and all.

FABRIC REQUIREMENTS

	Color	Yards	Inches	Centimeters
Fabric A	Alphabet Print	⅓ yd	12"	30.5cm
Fabric B	Pink Print	⅙ yd	6"	15.2cm
Fabric C	Yellow Dot	⅙ yd	6"	15.2cm
Fabric D	Mint Print	⅙ yd	6"	15.2cm

SUPPLIES

- 15" x 15" (38.1 x 38.1cm) needled cotton batting
- 12" x 12" (30.5 x 30.5cm) crinkle material
- Light pink thread
- ⅓ yard (30.5cm) pink flower trim
- Teether, small rattle, or anything a child would be interested in
- (3) 6" (15.2cm) long ribbons or as needed, for attaching to toy or teether
- (10) 5" (12.7cm) long ribbons or as needed, used as loops
- Needed tools (page 9)

CUTTING INSTRUCTIONS

	Amount Needed	Use
Fabric A	(2) 6" x 6" (15.2 x 15.2cm) squares	
	(1) 11" x 11" (27.9 x 27.9cm) square	backing fabric
Fabric B	(2) 2¼" x 6" (5.7 x 15.2cm) strips	
Fabric C	(2) 2¼" x 6" (5.7 x 15.2cm) strips	
Fabric D	(2) 2¼" x 6" (5.7 x 15.2cm) strips	
Batting	(4) 6" x 6" (15.2 x 15.2cm) squares	

Important

Make sure all ribbons, teethers, and toys are safe and approved for babies before using. The ribbons I used are double-side satin and grosgrain.

To launder the toy, clean in mild detergent by hand. Let air dry flat.

INSTRUCTIONS

1. Follow steps 2–4 of Flannel Baby Quilt (page 74) to make two Stripe blocks.

2. Pin 6" x 6" (15.2 x 15.2cm) Fabric A square to 6" x 6" (15.2 x 15.2cm) batting, wrong side down. Line up the corners. Starting at the bottom-left side, with design front and back upright, quilt vertical lines every ⅜" (1cm). Repeat to make one more Solid block.

ASSEMBLY

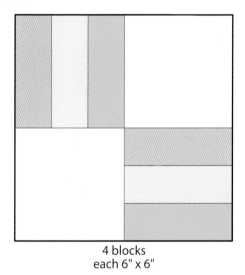

4 blocks
each 6" x 6"

3. Stitch the first-row blocks together, referring to Technique 1.

4. Repeat for the second row. Then join the two rows in the same way as step 3.

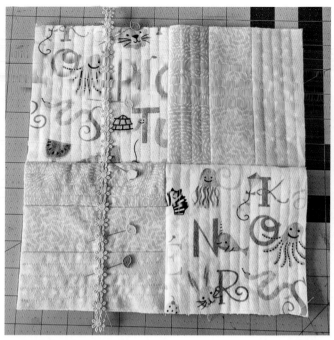

5. Stitch a length of pink flower trim to the front of the toy as shown.

6. Fold 5" (12.7cm) lengths of ribbon in half for a loop. Pin the loops around the sides. Arrange the raw edges along the outer edge of the toy as shown. More loops can be made with pink flower trim if desired. Slide the teethers and small toys onto the 6" (15.2cm) ribbon lengths. Fold those lengths back and pin. Stitch an ⅛" (3.2mm) seam around the edge to attach the ribbons.

FINISHING

8. Sew around the toy, leaving 3" (7.6cm) open on one side. Clip the corners. Flip the toy inside out, and shape the corners with a blunt-point instrument.

9. Stitch all around the toy, ⅛" (3.2mm) from the edge. This will stabilize the outer edge and close the 3" (7.6cm) gap.

10. Quilt a diagonal line from the top-left corner to the bottom-right corner. Repeat from the bottom-left corner to the top-right corner. This keeps the crinkle fabric in place.

7. Pin the 11" x 11" (27.9 x 27.9cm) Fabric A square to the front of the quilted piece, right sides together. Keep the ribbons and toys between the two pieces of fabric. Pin the crinkle material on top of the backing fabric.

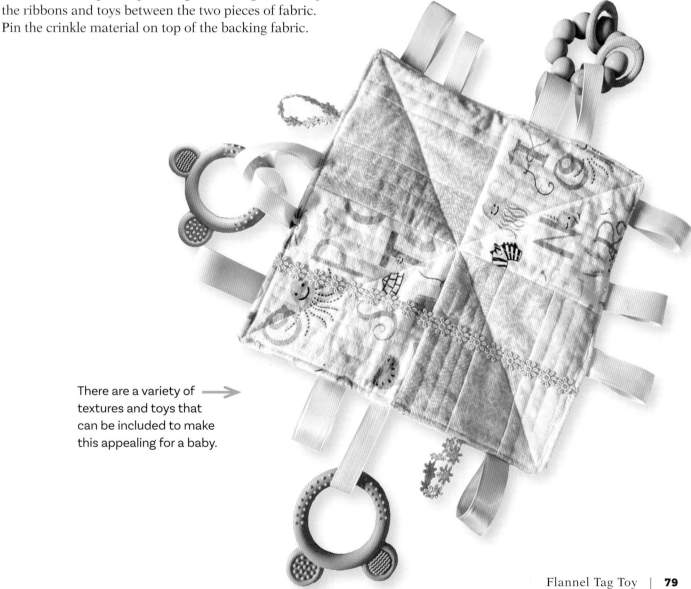

There are a variety of textures and toys that can be included to make this appealing for a baby.

Flannel Tag Toy | **79**

Lemur Play Mat

FINISHED SIZE: 28" x 36" (71.1 x 91.4cm)

My grandson, Camden, developed a love of lemurs a couple of years ago. I thought it would be fun to make a play mat with a lemur instead of a bear or bunny, although I love bears and bunnies too. Choose a fun color palette for your geometric play mat.

This project uses Joining Technique 4 (page 14) to piece the block front, batting, and backing at the same time. The pieces will be assembled by stitching the blocks back-to-back. On the front, a binding will be added to cover the seams.

FABRIC REQUIREMENTS

		Color	Yards	Inches	Centimeters
Fabric A		Blue Dot	½ yd	18"	45.7cm
Fabric B		Blue Circles	1 yd	36"	91.4cm
Fabric C		Green Dot	½ yd	18"	45.7cm
Fabric D		Green Swirls	1 yd	36"	91.4cm
Fabric E		Striped	½ yd	18"	45.7cm
Fabric F		White Dot	¼ yd	9"	22.9cm
Fabric G		Gray Dot	¼ yd	9"	22.9cm
Fabric H		Black	¼ yd	9"	22.9cm

SUPPLIES

- Lemur Templates (page 139)
- Crib-size needled cotton batting
- Blue thread
- Green thread
- White thread
- Black thread
- Quilt basting spray
- (3) ½" (1.3cm) white buttons
- (2) ³⁄₁₆" (4.8mm) amber buttons
- 5 yards (4.6m) thin white rickrack
- Iron-on adhesive
- Needed tools (page 9)

While I made a lemur, this quilt could be made with any animal.

CUTTING INSTRUCTIONS

Note: For all template pieces, attach the fabric to the iron-on adhesive first, then cut out. Follow manufacturer's instructions.

	Amount Needed	Use
Fabric A	(20) 2½" x 2½" (6.4 x 6.4cm) squares	
	(3) 3" x 9" (7.6 x 22.9cm) strips	
	(2) 3" x 7" (7.6 x 17.8cm) strips	
	(1) 6" x 9" (15.2 x 22.9cm) strip	backing fabric
	(2) 6" x 6" (15.2 x 15.2cm) squares	backing fabric
Fabric B	(20) 2½" x 2½" (6.4 x 6.4cm) squares	
	(3) 3" x 9" (7.6 x 22.9cm) strips	
	(2) 3" x 7" (7.6 x 17.8cm) strips	
	(3) 6" x 6" (15.2 x 15.2cm) squares	backing fabric
	(2) 6" x 9" (15.2 x 22.9cm) strips	backing fabric
	(2) 6" x 7" (15.2 x 17.8cm) strips	backing fabric
	(1) 22" x 22" (55.9 x 55.9cm) square	binding
Fabric C	(12) 2½" x 2½" (6.4 x 6.4cm) squares	
	(5) 3" x 9" (7.6 x 22.9cm) strips	
	(3) 3" x 7" (7.6 x 17.8cm) strips	
	(1) 6" x 6" (15.2 x 15.2cm) square	backing fabric
	(2) 6" x 9" (15.2 x 22.9cm) strips	backing fabric
Fabric D	(12) 2½" x 2½" (6.4 x 6.4cm) squares	
	(5) 3" x 9" (7.6 x 22.9cm) strips	
	(3) 3" x 7" (7.6 x 17.8cm) strips	
	(1) 12" x 15" (30.5 x 38.1cm) strip	
	(1) 12" x 15" (30.5 x 38.1cm) strip	backing fabric
	(2) 6" x 6" (15.2 x 15.2cm) squares	backing fabric

	Amount Needed	Use
	(3) 6" x 9" (15.2 x 22.9cm) strips	backing fabric
	(3) 6" x 7" (15.2 x 17.8cm) strips	backing fabric
Fabric E	(6) 3" x 3" (7.6 x 7.6cm) squares	
	1 Tail Front	lemur
	1 Tail Back	lemur
	(1) 18" x 18" (45.7 x 45.7cm) square	bias tape
Fabric F	1 Face	lemur
	2 Outer Ears	lemur
	1 Stomach	lemur
	3 Balloons	lemur
Fabric G	2 Ears	lemur
	1 Head	lemur
	(4) 1" x 4" (2.5 x 10.2cm) strips	lemur
	1 Body	lemur
Fabric H	2 Inner Ears	lemur
	1 Nose	lemur
	4 Paws	lemur
	2 Eyes	lemur
Batting	(8) 6" x 6" (15.2 x 15.2cm) squares	
	(5) 6" x 7" (15.2 x 17.8cm) strips	
	(8) 6" x 9" (15.2 x 22.9cm) strips	
	(1) 12" x 15" (30.5 x 38.1cm) strip	

VERTICAL BLOCKS

1. Spray one side of the 6" x 9" (15.2 x 22.9cm) batting with basting spray. Lay the sticky side of the batting onto the wrong side of the 6" x 9" (15.2 x 22.9cm) Fabric D strip.

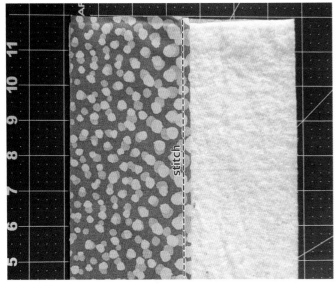

2. Place 3" x 9" (7.6 x 22.9cm) Fabric C strip on the left side of the batting vertically. Stitch 3" x 9" (7.6 x 22.9cm) Fabric D strip on top of the first strip, right sides together. Flip the fabric back and press the seam.

3. Repeat steps 1 and 2 to make four more blocks. Use Fabric C for the backing fabric on two blocks. The C backing will be for the bottom of the play mat.

4. Repeat steps 1 and 2 to make three more blocks. Use Fabric A and B strips for the pieced fronts. Use Fabric B for the backing fabric on two blocks and Fabric A for one block. The A backing will be for the bottom of the play mat.

5. Spray one side of the 6" x 7" (15.2 x 17.8cm) batting with basting spray. Lay the sticky side of the batting onto the wrong side of the 6" x 7" (15.2 x 17.8cm) Fabric D strip.

6. Place 3" x 7" (7.6 x 17.8cm) Fabric C strip on the left side of the batting vertically. Stitch 3" x 7" (7.6 x 17.8cm) Fabric D strip on top of the first strip, right sides together. Flip the fabric back and press the seam.

7. Repeat steps 5 and 6 to make two more C/D blocks.

8. Repeat steps 5 and 6 to make two more blocks. Use Fabric A and B strips for the pieced fronts and Fabric B for the backing fabric.

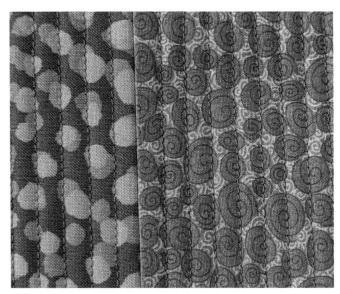

9. On the green blocks, use green thread to quilt vertical lines ⅜" (1cm) apart, moving from top to bottom. Repeat with blue thread on the blue blocks. Set blocks aside.

SQUARE BLOCKS

10. Spray one side of the 6" x 6" (15.2 x 15.2cm) batting with basting spray. Lay the sticky side of the batting onto the wrong side of the 6" x 6" (15.2 x 15.2cm) Fabric B strip.

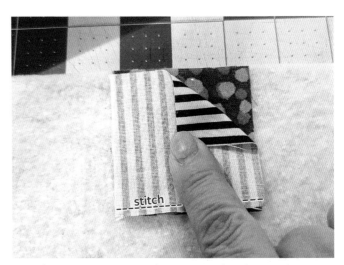

11. Place one 2½" x 2½" (6.4 x 6.4cm) Fabric A square along the top-center of the batting. Stitch 2½" x 2½" (6.4 x 6.4cm) Fabric E on top, right sides together, along the bottom edge. Flip the fabric down and press the seam.

12. Lay a second Fabric A square on top of the center square, and stitch the seam along the bottom. Flip and press.

Note

If desired, you can change the arrangement of the A/B and C/D squares. I mixed it up on a few Square blocks, but you may want a more uniform look.

13. Without batting, sew one 2½" x 2½" (6.4 x 6.4cm) B square to an A square. Stitch another B square to the opposite side of A. Press the seams flat. Repeat for another three-block unit.

14. Stitch one three-block unit on top of the strip in the center of the batting. Flip and press. Repeat with the other unit, for the other side of the block.

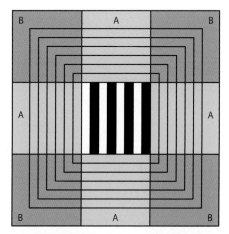

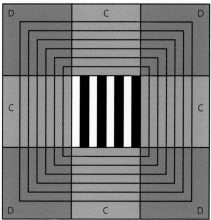

15. Repeat steps 10–14 to make four more A/B blocks. Use A as the backing for two blocks. Repeat steps 10–14 to make three C/D blocks, using D for the backing fabric on two blocks and C for one block. Quilt the squares with matching thread, following the diagram.

LEMUR BLOCK

16. Spray both sides of the 12" x 15" (30.5 x 38.1cm) batting with basting spray. Lay one sticky side of the batting onto the wrong side of one 12" x 15" (30.5 x 38.1cm) Fabric D strip. Then repeat with the second Fabric D strip on the front.

17. Remove all adhesive paper from the lemur pieces. Arrange the pieces in the center of the block, except for the Tail Back piece. Make sure to layer appropriately. Extend the Tail Front to the edge of the block, so it looks like it is going around the block. Press all pieces in place.

Tip

Before removing the adhesive paper, test your lemur arrangement. Make sure you like the pose and know which pieces sit on top of each other. You may want to label the pieces in numerical order to make it easier when placing the layers down.

18. Blanket stitch around the pieces, excluding the hands, feet, inner ears, eyes, and nose. Add zigzag-stitch whiskers on the face with black thread.

19. Place the Tail Back appliqué piece on the 12" x 15" (30.5 x 38.1cm) Fabric D rectangle, on the back, so that when the front and back are placed together, the tail looks as if it is going around the block to the back. Make sure it is positioned properly before pressing to secure. Blanket stitch around this tail section as well.

20. Quilt the Lemur block like the other vertical blocks: from top to bottom, spacing the lines ⅜" (1cm) apart, and using white thread.

ASSEMBLY

21. Lay the blocks out on a flat surface according to the Front Layout Diagram and Back Layout Diagram. Keep in mind that the different blocks of each kind are on the bottom, aligned with the Lemur block.

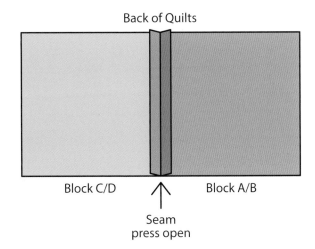

Back of Quilts

Block C/D   ↑   Block A/B

Seam
press open

22. Sew together the first (C/D) and second (A/B) blocks in the first row, using Joining Technique 4. Remember, this row is made of five 6" x 7" (15.2 x 17.8cm) Vertical blocks. Continue in this manner across the row.

23. Following the graphs and Technique 4, stitch each row. The second and fourth rows are Square blocks. The third and fifth rows are 6" x 9" (15.2 x 22.9cm) Vertical blocks.

24. Sew the first row to the second row, right sides together, matching the seams. Sew the third row to the second row. Sew the fourth row to the fifth rows. Sew the Lemur block to the end of the fourth and fifth row. Stitch the bottom piece to the top piece—third row to fourth row.

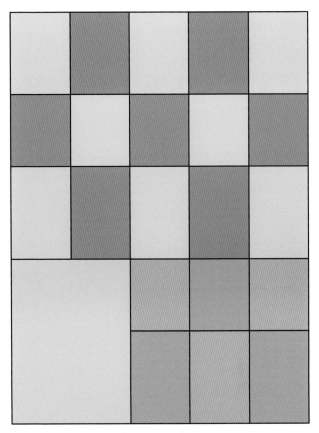

Back Layout Diagram

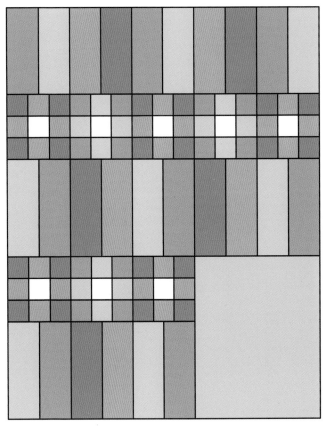

Front Layout Diagram

FINISHING

25. Use the 22" x 22" (55.9 x 55.9cm) Fabric B square to make binding. Pin and stitch to the back of the play mat, covering the vertical seam lines. Stitch close to the fold edges. When all vertical seams are covered, repeat for the horizontal seams.

26. Iron the balloons to the play mat according to the photos. Zigzag stitch around the edges of the balloons with white thread. Quilt random loops in the balloons to give texture.

27. Cut the rickrack into three appropriate lengths. Pin and sew them in place with white thread to serve as the balloon strings.

28. Stitch the amber buttons onto the eyes. Stitch one white button at the base of each balloon, covering where the rickrack ends.

29. Use the 18" x 18" (45.7 x 45.7cm) Fabric E square to make bias tape (page 16) for the perimeter. Attach the bias tape around the entire play mat.

Be careful when placing the rickrack. You want the balloon strings to look natural when collected in the lemur's paw.

Lemur Tote Bag

FINISHED SIZE: 7" x 14" (17.8 x 35.6cm)

This petite bag holds the rolled-up Lemur Play Mat snugly. Being such a simple design, this same pattern would be great for a bottle of wine or a baguette. A metal ring can easily attach teethers or other items like toys, rattles, and pacifiers. This ring can also be switched from this bag to your baby bag so those items can tag along.

FABRIC REQUIREMENTS

		Color	Yards	Inches	Centimeters
Fabric A		Blue Dot	¼ yd	9"	22.9cm
Fabric B		Blue Circles	½ yd	18"	45.7cm
Fabric C		Green Dot	¼ yd	9"	22.9cm
Fabric D		Green Swirls	½ yd	18"	45.7cm
Fabric E		Striped	¼ yd	9"	22.9cm

SUPPLIES

- 20" x 20" (50.8 x 50.8cm) needled cotton batting
- Green thread
- Blue thread
- Quilt basting spray
- 2 silver plastic grommets, 1½" (3.8cm) diameter
- Grommet template
- 3" (7.6cm) diameter metal stationary ring
- Teether, rattle, pacifier, or toy
- Needed tools (page 9)

CUTTING INSTRUCTIONS

	Amount Needed	Use
Fabric A	(20) 2½" x 2½" (6.4 x 6.4cm) squares	
Fabric B	(20) 2½" x 2½" (6.4 x 6.4cm) squares	
	(5) 6" x 6" (15.2 x 15.2cm) squares	backing fabric
	(1) 10" x 10" (25.4 x 25.4cm) square	bias tape
Fabric C	(16) 2½" x 2½" (6.4 x 6.4cm) squares	
Fabric D	(16) 2½" x 2½" (6.4 x 6.4cm) squares	
	(4) 6" x 6" (15.2 x 15.2cm) squares	backing fabric
	(1) 4" x 20" (10.2 x 50.8cm) strip	shoulder strap
Fabric E	(9) 2½" x 2½" (6.4 x 6.4cm) squares	
Batting	(9) 6" x 6" (15.2 x 15.2cm) squares	

INSTRUCTIONS

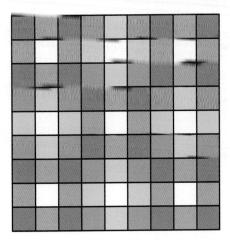

1. Follow steps 10–14 of Lemur Play Mat (page 83) to make nine Square blocks. Make five with A/B squares on the front and Fabric B on the back. Make four with C/D squares on the front and Fabric D on the back. Lay out the blocks according to the diagram.

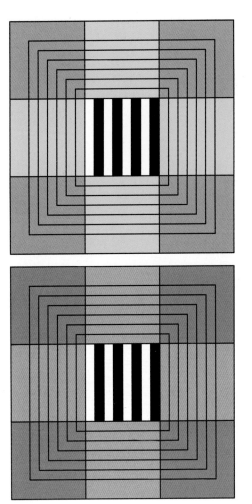

2. Quilt the squares with matching thread. For my blocks, I stitched boxes ¼" (6.4mm) apart from the center out. Return the blocks to their arrangement.

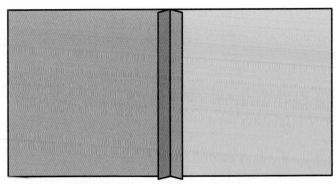

3. Sew the first and second blocks in the first row, right sides together. Sew the third block to the second in the same way. Iron the seams open and flat.

4. Repeat for the other two rows. Sew the rows together, matching seams and stitching with right sides together.

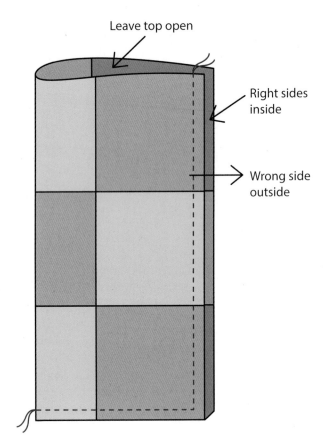

Leave top open

Right sides inside

Wrong side outside

5. Fold the pieced front in half, right sides together, and pin to make a tube. Sew the side and bottom. Flip the bag inside out.

ASSEMBLY & FINISHING

6. Use the 10" x 10" (25.4 x 25.4cm) Fabric B square to make ½" (1.2cm) double-fold bias tape (page 16). Sew the bias tape to the opening edge of the bag.

7. Draw a circle, using the template from the grommets, on each side of the bag. Cut the grommet hole open, and insert the grommet back from behind, according to instructions with grommet packaging. Secure by pressing the grommet front onto the back piece with force through the hole.

8. Use the 4" x 20" (10.2 x 50.8cm) Fabric D strip to make a shoulder strap (page 20).

9. Insert one end of a strap into one grommet hole from the front of the bag. Fold that end over by ¼" (6.4mm) twice, enclosing the raw edge. Stitch this folded end of the handle close to the top of the bag. Repeat for the other end of the strap.

10. Attach metal ring to the strap to hold the toys and teethers.

Brown Button Throw Quilt

Looking for a cozy throw quilt on a cool fall day? Look no further than this autumn beauty. Fifty-four squares comprised of five slanted stripes each are sewn together with a lattice on the front to accentuate the rotating patchwork.

This project uses Joining Technique 4 (page 14) to piece the block front, batting, and backing at the same time. The pieces will be assembled by stitching the blocks back-to-back. On the front, a binding will be added to cover the seams. The quilting is a series of lines that are stitched ¼" (6.4mm) apart and following the slanted strip lines.

FABRIC REQUIREMENTS

	Color		Yards	Inches	Centimeters
Fabric A		Rust Dash	1¾ yds	63"	160cm
Fabric B		Ivory Floral	1½ yds	54"	137.2cm
Fabric C		Gold Floral	1½ yds	54"	137.2cm
Fabric D		Brown Floral	1⅓ yds	48"	121.9cm
Fabric E		Brown Dot	1½ yds	54"	137.2cm
Fabric F		Brown Print	¾ yd	27"	68.6cm

SUPPLIES

- 40" x 60" (101.6 x 152.4cm) needled cotton batting
- 2–3 spools brown thread
- Quilt basting spray
- 162 natural buttons, ⅜" (1cm) diameter
- Needed tools (page 9)

CUTTING INSTRUCTIONS

	Amount Needed	Use
Fabric A	(18) 6½" x 6½" (16.5 x 16.5cm) squares	backing fabric
	(54) 2½" x 8" (6.4 x 20.3cm) strips	
Fabric B	(12) 6½" x 6½" (16.5 x 16.5cm) squares	backing fabric
	(54) 2½" x 8" (6.4 x 20.3cm) strips	
Fabric C	(12) 6½" x 6½" (16.5 x 16.5cm) squares	backing fabric
	(54) 2½" x 8" (6.4 x 20.3cm) strips	
Fabric D	(54) 2½" x 8" (6.4 x 20.3cm) strips	
Fabric E	(12) 6½" x 6½" (16.5 x 16.5cm) squares	backing fabric
	(54) 2½" x 8" (6.4 x 20.3cm) strips	
Fabric F	(1) 21" x 21" (53.3 x 53.3cm) square	binding
Batting	(54) 6" x 6" (15.2 x 15.2cm) squares	

INSTRUCTIONS

1. Separate the cut fabric pieces into piles for each block. Gather one piece of batting, one 6½" x 6½" (16.5 x 16.5cm) backing fabric, and one of each of the five 2½" x 8" (6.4 x 20.3cm) fabric strips.

2. Spray one side of the 6" x 6" (15.2 x 15.2cm) batting with basting spray. Lay the sticky side of the batting onto the wrong side of the 6" x 6" (15.2 x 15.2cm) backing fabric square.

3. Place one fabric strip on the batting along an edge. Lay a second strip on top, right sides together, at a slight slant. Stitch through the batting and backing. Flip the fabric back and press the seam.

4. Stitch another fabric strip, right sides together, with the last. Place at a slight angle to the last. Flip the fabric and press the seam.

5. Repeat two more times. The fifth strip should cover the opposite edge, and all strips should be angled against each other. Flip the block over and trim fabric to the batting edge. Spray basting spray under the first and last strip to secure the batting for quilting.

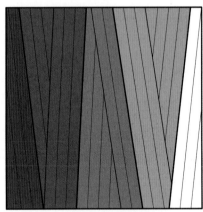
Quilted Block

6. To quilt the block, stitch straight lines that are ¼" (6.4mm) away from the seam of each strip. Some lines may meet at a point or cross each other as shown in the illustration.

7. Sew buttons onto all 54 blocks, grouping them into lines of three same-color buttons.

ASSEMBLY & FINISHING

8. Lay out the blocks in nine rows of six blocks. Alternate vertical and horizontal striped blocks on the front. If desired, you can also arrange blocks so that the backing fabric creates a stripe design as shown above. Follow this fabric order: A, E, C, B, A, E, C, B, A.

9. Sew together the first and second blocks in the first row, using Joining Technique 4. Continue in this manner across the row.

10. Repeat for all nine rows. Stitch the rows together in the same way, matching seams and checking the rows on the back.

11. Use the 21" x 21" (53.3 x 53.3cm) Fabric F square to make bias tape (page 16). On the front of the quilt, pin one strip of binding to cover a horizontal seam. Repeat for all rows. Then complete the vertical seams.

12. Bind the edge with the remaining bias tape to complete.

Brown Button Lumbar Pillow

When you curl up with the Brown Button Throw Quilt on a cool fall day, you will need a pillow for your back or to rest your arm on. The pillow is made using the same blocks and buttons for a comfy ensemble.

This project uses Joining Technique 4 (page 14) to piece the layers at the same time. Because this is a pillow, we are not using a backing fabric. The pieces will be assembled by stitching the blocks back-to-back. On the front, a binding will be added to cover the seams.

FABRIC REQUIREMENTS

	Color		Yards	Inches	Centimeters
Fabric A		Rust Dash	¼ yd	9"	22.9cm
Fabric B		Ivory Floral	¼ yd	9"	22.9cm
Fabric C		Gold Floral	¼ yd	9"	22.9cm
Fabric D		Brown Print	½ yd	18"	45.7cm
Fabric E		Brown Dot	¼ yd	9"	22.9cm

SUPPLIES

- 40" x 60" (101.6 x 152.4cm) needled cotton batting
- Brown thread
- Quilt basting spray
- 24 natural buttons, ⅜" (1cm) diameter
- Invisible zipper (optional)
- 12" x 20" (30.5 x 50.8cm) pillow form
- Needed tools (page 9)

CUTTING INSTRUCTIONS

	Amount Needed	Use
Fabric A	(16) 2½" x 8" (6.4 x 20.3cm) strips	
Fabric B	(8) 2½" x 8" (6.4 x 20.3cm) strips	
Fabric C	(16) 2½" x 8" (6.4 x 20.3cm) strips	
Fabric D	(1) 16" x 16" (40.6 x 40.6cm) square	binding
Fabric E	(16) 2½" x 8" (6.4 x 20.3cm) strips	
Batting	(16) 6" x 6" (15.2 x 15.2cm) squares	

The buttons add a fun detail to this pillow, but you do not need to include if you find them uncomfortable to rest on.

FRONT OF THE PILLOW

1. Separate the cut fabric pieces into piles for each front block. Gather one piece of batting and one of each of the four 2½" x 8" (6.4 x 20.3cm) fabric strips.

2. Follow steps 3–6 of Brown Button Throw Quilt (page 94) to make eight blocks. Instead using five slanted strips, this block uses four.

3. Sew buttons onto all eight blocks, grouping them into lines of three same-color buttons as shown above.

BACK OF THE PILLOW

4. Lay one 2½" x 8" (6.4 x 20.3cm) Fabric A, C, or E strip on the batting along an edge. Stitch another random strip on top of the first, right sides together. Flip the fabric back and press the seam. Stitch a final strip to the batting to complete this block. Use only one strip of each color in the block. These strips will be sewn straight to each other, not slanted as before.

5. Repeat to make seven more blocks. Square them. Quilt the blocks with straight lines ⅜" (1cm) apart, following the direction of the strips.

ASSEMBLY & FINISHING

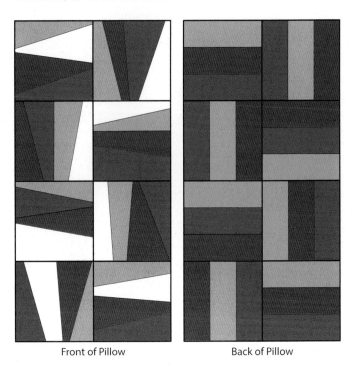

Front of Pillow   Back of Pillow

6. Lay out the 16 blocks according to the diagrams for the front and back of the pillow. Alternate vertical and horizontal striped blocks.

7. Sew together the two blocks in the first row, using Joining Technique 4. Continue in this manner for all four rows.

8. Stitch the rows together in the same way, matching seams, for a completed pillow front.

9. Use the 16" x 16" (40.6 x 40.6cm) Fabric D square to make bias tape. Stitch this binding between the rows first, then one strip vertically between the columns.

10. Repeat steps 7 and 8 for the back of the pillow. Then use the remaining bias tape to bind the seams, as in step 9, as shown in the right photo.

11. If desired, insert the invisible zipper (page 18) along one of the long sides between the pillow front and back.

12. Sew the front and back of the pillow, right sides together. If not using a zipper, leave 7" (17.8cm) opening on one long side. Cut the corners. Flip the pillow inside out and push out the corners.

13. If using a zipper, pull the pillow form through the opening. If not using a zipper, insert the pillow, then close the opening on the side by hand stitching.

Using only warm colors on the back creates a subtle change, but it's just as lovely as the pillow front.

Simplified Cathedral Window Tote Bag

FINISHED SIZE: 13" x 13" (33 x 33cm)

In this project, we'll be completing a tote bag by using the faux-cathedral-window concept. The sides are joined in a way to complete the circles all the way around. The bag is gusseted to create more space inside. This simplified cathedral window design is so much fun to do. I enjoy each step, and watching it come together is rewarding; it looks difficult, but we know better.

There is no batting in this project, but the technique of sewing the front and back at the same time is similar to QAYG. The fabric I used in this project is Carnival Quilting Fabric by Happy Blooms by Sue Penn.

FABRIC REQUIREMENTS

	Color		Yards	Inches	Centimeters
Fabric A		Multicolor Print	1½ yds	54"	137.2cm
Fabric B		Lime Green	1 fat quarter	18" x 21"	45.7 x 53.3cm
Fabric C		Salmon	1 fat quarter	18" x 21"	45.7 x 53.3cm
Fabric D		Blue	1 fat quarter	18" x 21"	45.7 x 53.3cm
Fabric E		Mustard	1 fat quarter	18" x 21"	45.7 x 53.3cm

SUPPLIES

- Thread of your choice
- 1 yard (91.4cm) iron-on adhesive
- 3½" x 3½" (8.9 x 8.9cm) cardboard square
- 5" (12.7cm) diameter cardboard circle
- 18 green buttons, ½" (1.3cm) diameter
- 4 green buttons, 1¼" (3.2cm) diameter
- Needed tools (page 9)

CUTTING INSTRUCTIONS

	Amount Needed	Use
Fabric A	(4) 18" x 18" (45.7 x 45.7cm) squares	
	(1) 12" x 12" (30.5 x 30.5cm) square	bias tape
Fabric B	(1) 18" x 18" (45.7 x 45.7cm) square	
Fabric C	(1) 18" x 18" (45.7 x 45.7cm) square	
	(2) 6" x 33" (15.2 x 83.8cm) strips	shoulder straps
Fabric D	(1) 18" x 18" (45.7 x 45.7cm) square	
Fabric E	(1) 18" x 18" (45.7 x 45.7cm) square	
Iron-On Adhesive	(4) 18" x 18" (45.7 x 45.7cm) squares	

INSTRUCTIONS

1. Iron one piece of adhesive to the wrong side of one 18" x 18" (45.7 x 45.7cm) Fabric A square. Repeat for the other three pieces of iron-on adhesive and Fabric A.

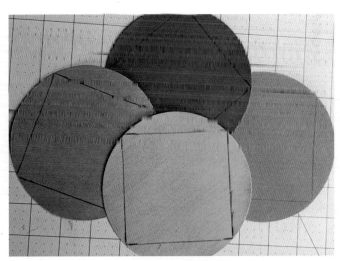

4. Place the cardboard square on any solid-color circle. Make sure that all four corners of the square are inside the circle. Trace around the square with a pencil or marker. Repeat on all solid circles. This line will be covered in a later step.

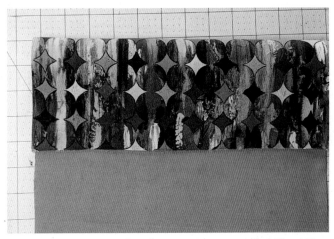

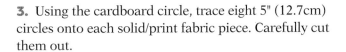

2. Iron one prepared Fabric A piece to each 18" x 18" (45.7 x 45.7cm) Fabric B, C, D, and E squares, wrong sides together. This should adhere the fabrics together.

3. Using the cardboard circle, trace eight 5" (12.7cm) circles onto each solid/print fabric piece. Carefully cut them out.

5. Lay the colored circles out on the workspace according to the Bag Layout Diagram (page 104).

Alternative to Cardboard

I used a die-cutting machine to make these circles, which made everything a lot easier. If this is an option for you, use a 5" (12.7cm) circle die to cut out eight circles each for Fabrics B, C, D, and E with Fabric A on the back for all. Be incredibly careful when cutting not to cut off any circle edges.

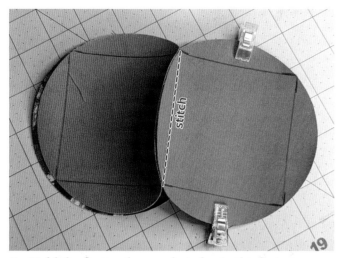

6. Hold the first and second circles in the first row together, print to print. Line up the corners of the squares to match. Pin or clip the circles to hold. Stitch along the pencil line of one solid-color circle.

7. Repeat for the third and fourth circles in the first row. Stitch the pairs together to complete the four-circle row. Iron all the flaps open and flat.

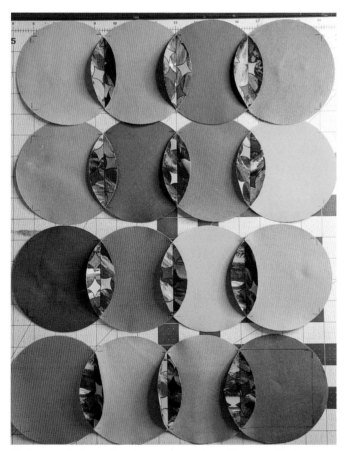

8. Repeat steps 6 and 7 to complete the remaining three rows.

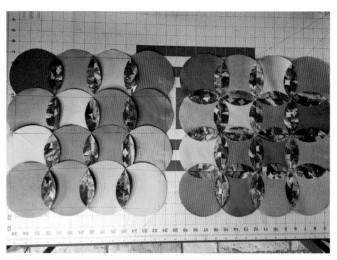

9. Stitch the first row to the second row, matching circles and seams along the pencil line. Repeat for remaining rows.

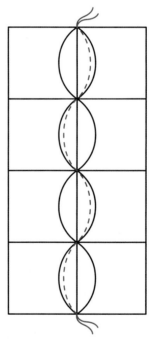

10. Iron the flaps of the joined rows open. Quilt ¼" (6.5mm) from the outer edges of the flaps, moving from one side to the other as shown. Do not stitch the flaps down.

11. Sew one button into the corners where four circles meet. Use nine ½" (1.3cm) diameter buttons.

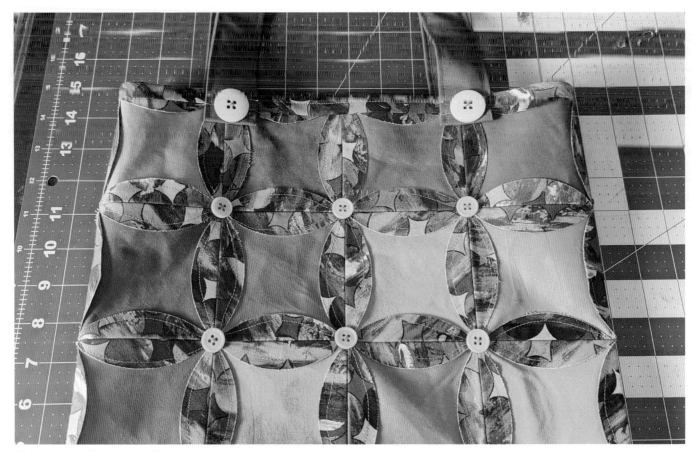

The bold multicolor print lends even more interest to this fun bag.

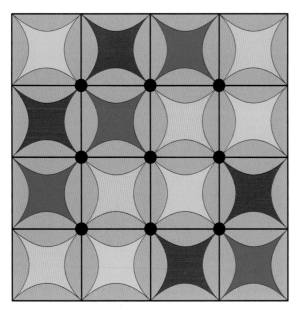

Bag Layout Diagram

12. Repeat steps 6–11 for the other 16 colored circles. This is the other side of the tote bag.

ASSEMBLY & FINISHING

13. Pin or clip the two sides of the tote bag together, Fabric A circles together, matching all seams. Stitch together along the lines on the squares. Iron the flaps and quilt side flaps. Flip bag inside out, facing colored circles together.

14. Determine which end is the bottom of the bag. On that end, stitch ¼" (6.4mm) in from the circle seams, ensuring it closes the bottom completely. Trim excess flaps away from the seam.

15. Stitch 1½" (3.8cm) gussets in the corners of the bottom (page 21). After trimming threads, flip the bag inside out again.

16. Iron the top edge flaps flat to the outside of the bag. Quilt a design on the flaps.

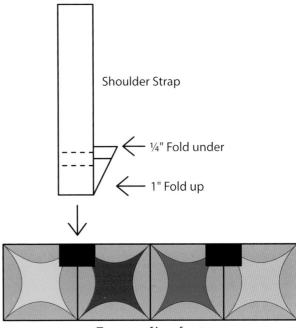

Shoulder Strap

← ¼" Fold under

← 1" Fold up

Top row of bag front

17. Use the 12" x 12" (30.5 x 30.5cm) Fabric A square to make bias tape (page 16). Stitch the bias tape around the top edge of the tote bag.

18. Use 6" x 33" (15.2 x 83.8cm) Fabric C strip to make a shoulder strap (page 20). Repeat for second strap.

19. Fold one end of one strap under ¼" (6.4mm), then fold over 1" (2.5cm). Stitch in place ¼" (6.4mm) from the end of the strap. Stitch another line ¼" (6.4mm) away from the first. Repeat on the other end of the same strap, making sure not to twist the strap.

20. Sew a 1¼" (3.2cm) diameter button to the end of each handle.

21. Repeat steps 19 and 20 for the strap on the other side.

Cathedral Table Mat

FINISHED SIZE: 12" x 12" (30.5 x 30.5cm)

In this project, we will be completing a centerpiece mat by using faux cathedral windows. The center of the design is cut away for a doily appearance. This table centerpiece may look hard to make, but it is easy.

Just like Simplified Cathedral Window Tote Bag, there is no batting in this project, but the technique of sewing the front and back at the same time is like QAYG. The fabric I used in this project is Carnival Quilting Fabric by Happy Blooms by Sue Penn.

FABRIC REQUIREMENTS

	Color		Yards	Inches	Centimeters
Fabric A		Multicolor Print	⅔ yd	24"	61cm
Fabric B		Lime Green	1 fat quarter	18" x 21"	45.7 x 53.3cm
Fabric C		Salmon	1 fat quarter	18" x 21"	45.7 x 53.3cm
Fabric D		Blue	1 fat quarter	18" x 21"	45.7 x 53.3cm
Fabric E		Mustard	1 fat quarter	18" x 21"	45.7 x 53.3cm

SUPPLIES
- Thread of your choice
- 18" x 48" (45.7 x 121.9cm) iron-on adhesive
- 3½" x 3½" (8.9 x 8.9cm) cardboard square
- 5" (12.7cm) diameter cardboard circle
- 8 red buttons, ⅜" (1cm) diameter
- Needed tools (page 9)

CUTTING INSTRUCTIONS

	Amount Needed
Fabric A	(4) 12" x 18" (30.5 x 45.7cm) strips
Iron-On Adhesive	(4) 12" x 18" (30.5 x 45.7cm) strips

While the front of this mat is the the most interesting, I also love how it looks from the back.

INSTRUCTIONS

1. Iron one piece of adhesive to the wrong side of one 12" x 18" (30.5 x 45.7cm) Fabric A strip. Repeat for the other three pieces of iron-on adhesive and fabric.

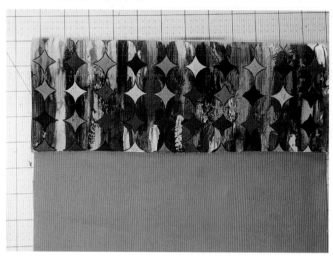

2. Iron one Fabric A piece to each 18" x 21" (45.7 x 53.3cm) Fabric B, C, D, and E square, wrong sides together. Trim the excess solid-color fabric.

3. Using the cardboard circle, trace four 5" (12.7cm) circles onto each solid/print fabric piece. Carefully cut them out.

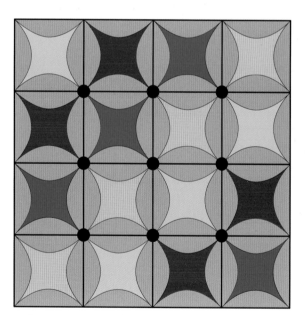

4. Follow steps 4–9 of Simplified Cathedral Window Tote Bag (page 102) to make one four by four circle layout.

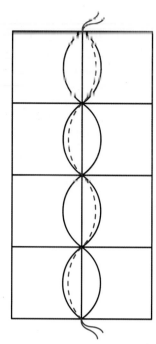

5. Iron the flaps of the joined rows open. Quilt ¼" (6.5mm) from the outer edges of the flaps, moving from one side to the other as shown. Finish the outside edges this way.

6. Carefully cut away the fabric of the four center circles.

7. Sew one button into the corners where four circles meet.

Whimsical Wall Hanging

FINISHED SIZE: 36" x 42" (91.4 x 106.7cm)

Wall hangings are decorations that show off artwork and quilted creations. Since this quilt won't need to be laundered, I've added some wooden embellishments at the top and bottom that are unexpected and add to the dimension of the quilt.

This project uses Joining Technique 4 (page 14) to piece the block front, batting, and backing at the same time. The pieces will be assembled by stitching the blocks back-to-back. On the front, a binding will be added to cover the seams. The fabrics I used in this project are by P. Carter Carpin of Serious Whimsey.

FABRIC REQUIREMENTS

	Color		Yards	Inches	Centimeters
Fabric A		Birdvine Ivory	1 yd	36"	91.4cm
Fabric B		Striped	1 yd	36"	91.4cm
Fabric C		Sunflower Cheesecloth	1 yd	36"	91.4cm
Fabric D		Salmon	1 yd	36"	91.4cm
Fabric E		Blue Dots	1¼ yds	45"	114.3cm

SUPPLIES

- 48" x 36" (121.9 x 91.4cm) needled cotton batting
- Thread of your choice
- Quilt basting spray
- 36" (91.4cm) wooden dowel, ½" (1.3cm) diameter
- 2 decorative wooden curtain finials, fitting the ends of the dowel
- 6 wooden beads, ¾" (1.9cm) diameter
- 4 wooden half beads, ¾" (1.9cm) diameter
- Off-white acrylic paint and paintbrush, or color of your choice
- Clear sealer for paint
- Wood or craft glue
- 4 snaps, ½" (1.3cm) diameter
- Iron-on adhesive tape
- Needed tools (page 9)

Tip

If you use a fabric with a definite direction to the print, you will want to be mindful of the placement of the fabric throughout this project.

CUTTING INSTRUCTIONS

	Amount Needed	Use
Fabric A	(9) 6½" x 6½" (16.5 x 16.5cm) squares, fussy cut if using a large print	
Fabric B	(9) 4½" x 12½" (11.4 x 31.8cm) strips	
	(9) 2½" x 6½" (6.4 x 16.5cm) strips	
	(3) 2" x 12" (5.1 x 30.5cm) strips	
Fabric C	(3) 12½" x 12½" (31.8 x 31.8cm) squares	backing fabric
	(3) 4½" x 6½" (11.4 x 16.5cm) strips	
	(3) 2½" x 12½" (6.4 x 31.8cm) strips	
	(1) 7" x 13" (17.8 x 33cm) strip	
Fabric D	(3) 12½" x 12½" (31.8 x 31.8cm) squares	backing fabric
	(3) 4½" x 6½" (11.4 x 16.5cm) strips	
	(3) 2½" x 12½" (6.4 x 31.8cm) strips	
	(4) 2" x 40" (5.1 x 101.6cm) strips	binding
	(1) 7" x 13" (17.8 x 33cm) strip	
Fabric E	(3) 12½" x 12½" (31.8 x 31.8cm) squares	backing fabric
	(3) 4½" x 6½" (11.4 x 16.5cm) strips	
	(3) 2½" x 12½" (6.4 x 31.8cm) strips	
	(1) 7" x 13" (17.8 x 33cm) strip	
	(1) 18" x 18" (45.7 x 45.7cm) square	bias tape
	(4) 6" x 6" (15.2 x 15.2cm) squares	tabs
Batting	(9) 12½" x 12½" (31.8 x 31.8cm) squares	
	(9) 6" x 6" (15.2 x 15.2cm) squares	

INSTRUCTIONS

1. Spray one side of the 6" x 6" (15.2 x 15.2cm) batting with basting spray. Lay the sticky side of the batting onto the wrong side of the 6½" x 6½" (16.5 x 16.5cm) Fabric A square. Make sure it's centered. Repeat for eight more. Set aside.

2. Spray one side of the 12½" x 12½" (31.8 x 31.8cm) batting with basting spray. Lay the sticky side of the batting onto the wrong side of the 12½" x 12½" (31.8 x 31.8cm) Fabric C square.

3. Place 2½" x 6½" (6.4 x 16.5cm) Fabric B strip on the bottom edge of the batting, arranged 1¾" (4.4cm) from right edge. Place a prepared square from step 1 on the Fabric B strip, right sides together, with the design upside down. Stitch along the top edge of the two fabrics. Flip the padded motif back and press the seam.

stitch

4. Place 4½" x 6½" (11.4 x 16.5cm) Fabric C strip, right sides together, on top of the last piece added. Make sure the sides are matched, then stitch. Flip the fabric and press the seam.

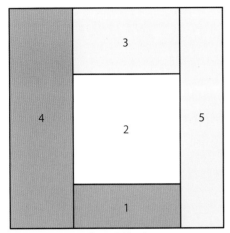

Fabric C Blocks
Make 3

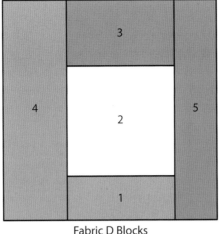

Fabric D Blocks
Make 3

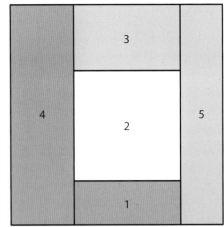

Fabric E Blocks
Make 3

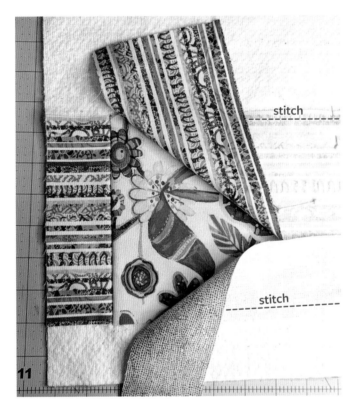

5. Stitch 4½" x 12½" (11.4 x 31.8cm) Fabric B strip, right sides together, to the unit. Stitch 2½" x 12½" (6.4 x 31¾") Fabric C strip, right sides together, to the unit. Flip and press both seams. Pin the fabrics in place on the perimeter, or use basting spray to hold the fabrics in place for quilting. The block has now been fully pieced.

6. Repeat steps 2–5 to make two more Fabric C blocks.

7. Repeat steps 2–5 to make three Fabric D blocks by swapping out the Fabric C pieces for Fabric D. Fabric B stays the same.

8. Repeat steps 2–5 to make three Fabric E blocks by swapping out the Fabric C pieces for Fabric E. Fabric B stays the same.

9. Quilt all the blocks according to the diagram below.

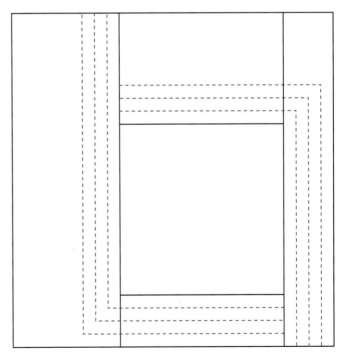

Quilting Diagram

Whimsical Wall Hanging | **113**

ASSEMBLY

10. Lay out the blocks visually according to the diagram. Fabric C is in the first column, Fabric E in the second, and Fabric D in the third.

11. Sew together the first and second blocks in the first row, using Joining Technique 4. Continue in this manner across the row. Press seams flat.

12. Repeat for two more rows. Press all seams flat. Stitch the first and second row together in the same way, matching all seams. Repeat with the second and third rows. Press all seams flat.

13. Make 1" (2.5cm) bias tape using the 2" x 40" (5.1 x 101.6cm) Fabric D strips, following step 6 of the bias tape instructions (page 16). Iron adhesive tape to the back.

14. Position the prepared bias tape over the vertical seams between the columns of blocks from the top to the bottom of the quilt. Ensure straight placement and press to activate adhesive tape. Stitch an ⅛" (3.2mm) seam on both fold edges of the bias tape to secure.

15. Repeat step 14, placing the bias tape on the horizontal seams between the rows.

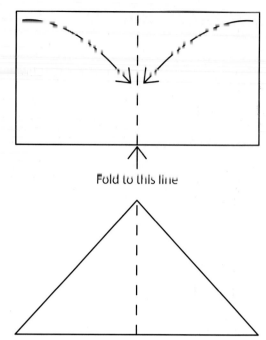

Fold to this line

16. Fold one long edge of 7" x 13" (17.8 x 33cm) Fabric C strip with both sides to the center, as shown. Stitch on each side of the center fold, ⅛" (3.2mm) from the fold. This creates a point for the quilt. Repeat with the Fabric D and E strips.

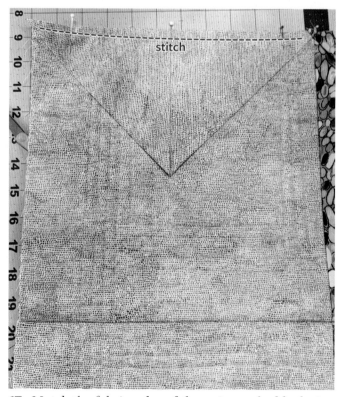

17. Match the fabric color of the point to the blocks in each column (C, D, or E). Stitch the folded triangles to the bottom of the quilt, wrong sides together. The seam should be on the front. Iron the seams open.

FINISHING

18. Use the 18" x 18" (45.7 x 45.7cm) Fabric E square to make ½" (1.2cm) double-fold bias tape. Stitch the bias around the left side, across the top, and down the right side. Across the bottom, stitch as bias tape (open).

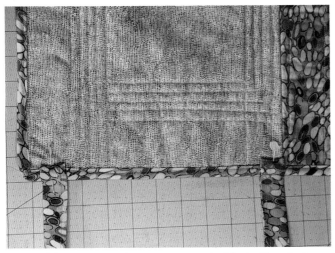

19. Fold one 4" x 6" (10.2 x 15.2cm) Fabric E strip in half (2" [5.1cm] wide). Iron the crease. Open the strip, and fold the long sides to the crease. Press and stitch along the new folds using the same technique on page 71. These will be the tabs at the top to hold the dowel in place. Make three more tabs.

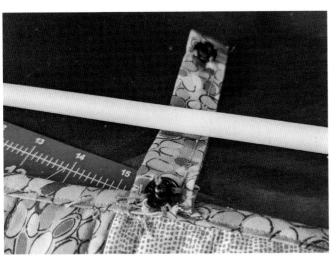

20. Stitch the tabs to the back top of the wall hanging, as shown. Hand stitch the snaps at each end of the tabs.

21. Paint the wood dowel, beads, and finials. Allow it to dry completely, and then paint with a second coat. Once dry, brush a clear sealer on the wooden pieces to protect the paint. Let dry. Use craft glue or wood glue to attach the finial ends to the dowel.

22. Make three strips of bias tape from the 2" x 12" (5.1 x 30.5cm) Fabric B strips. Slide two wooden beads onto the bottom of each strip, and tie a knot at the end. Sew these strips to the quilt banner down the center from the bias tape to the point. The beads will hang lower than the quilt.

23. Attach the quilt to the dowel with the tab snaps. Glue the half round wooden beads to the front of the quilt at the bottom of each fabric tab.

Whimsical Beaded Pillow

This pillow is a companion piece to the Whimsical Wall Hanging, constructed in a similar way with a couple more strips added to bring the block size up. The fabrics I used in this project are by P. Carter Carpin of Serious Whimsey. Look closely: It is beaded with tiny little glass beads for a special dimension and appeal.

FABRIC REQUIREMENTS

	Color	Yards	Inches	Centimeters
Fabric A	Birdvine Ivory	¼ yd	9"	22.9cm
Fabric B	Striped	¼ yd	9"	22.9cm
Fabric C	Sunflower Cheesecloth	⅓ yd	12"	30.5cm
Fabric D	Blue Dots	¼ yd	9"	22.9cm

SUPPLIES

- 18" x 36" (45.7 x 91.4cm) needled cotton batting
- Thread of your choice
- Quilt basting spray
- Tiny glass beads and a beading needle
- 16" x 16" (40.6 x 40.6cm) pillow form
- Needed tools (page 9)

CUTTING INSTRUCTIONS

	Amount Needed
Fabric A	(1) 6½" x 6½" (16.5 x 16.5cm) square
	(2) 6" x 16" (15.2 x 40.6cm) strips
Fabric B	(1) 4½" x 12½" (11.4 x 31.8cm) strip
	(1) 4½" x 16" (11.4 x 40.6cm) strip
	(1) 2½" x 6½" (6.4 x 16.5cm) strip
Fabric C	(1) 4½" x 6½" (11.4 x 16.5cm) strip
	(2) 2½" x 12½" (6.4 x 31.8cm) strips
	(1) 2¼" x 16" (5.7 x 40.6cm) strip
Fabric D	(1) 2¼" x 16" (5.7 x 40.6cm) strip
	(1) 2¼" x 18½" (5.7 x 47cm) strip
Batting	(2) 16" x 16" (40.6 x 40.6cm) squares
	(1) 12" x 12" (30.5 x 30.5cm) square
	(2) 5" x 5" (12.7 x 12.7cm) squares

FRONT OF THE PILLOW

1. Spray one side of the 6" x 6" (15.2 x 15.2cm) batting with basting spray. Lay the sticky side of the batting onto the wrong side of the 6⅛" x 6⅛" (16.5 x 16.5cm) Fabric A square. Make sure its centered.

2. Follow steps 3–5 of Whimsical Wall Hanging (page 112) to make one pieced block.

3. Quilt the block according to the diagram below.

4. Using the beading needle and tiny glass beads, stitch a random design onto the print. Adorn as heavily as desired.

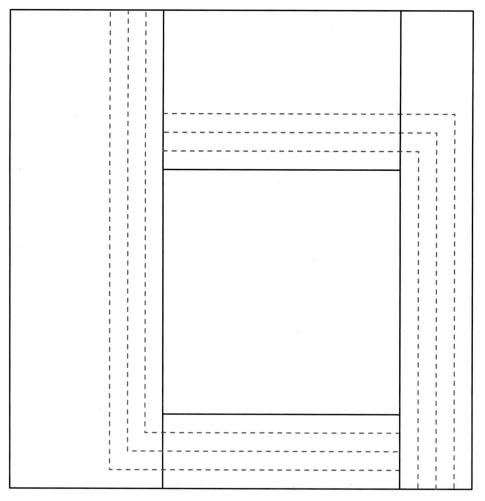

Quilting Diagram

5. Place the pieced and quilted block in the center of the 16" x 16" (40.6 x 40.6cm) batting. Place the second 2½" x 12½" (6.4 x 31.8cm) Fabric C strip to the left side of the block, right sides together, and stitch in place.

6. Attach 2¼" x 16" (5.7 x 40.6cm) Fabric C strip across the bottom, in the same manner. Attach 2¼" x 16" (5.7 x 40.6cm) Fabric D strip down the right side. Attach 2¼" x 18½" (5.7 x 47cm) Fabric D strip across the top. Leave the corners in place, and sew over for stronger corners.

BACK OF THE PILLOW

7. Place a 6" x 16" (15.2 x 40.6cm) Fabric A strip to the left side of 16" x 16" (40.6 x 40.6cm) batting, wrong side down. Place 4½" x 16" (11.4 x 40.6cm) Fabric B strip on top, right sides together, and stitch. Flip Fabric B and press.

8. Place the second 6" x 16" (15.2 x 40.6cm) Fabric A strip to Fabric B, right sides together, and stitch. Fold Fabric A back. There is no quilting on the back of the pillow.

ASSEMBLY & FINISHING

9. Square the pillow front and pillow back. Stitch with right sides together, matching the corners. Leave an opening of 8" (20.3cm). Clip the corners.

10. Flip the pillow inside out, push out the corners, and iron the seams. Insert the pillow form, and work it into the corners and the pillow cover evenly. Stitch the opening shut by hand.

Memory Quilt

Shortly after my father, Ed, passed away, my sister and I made quilt pieces from his everyday shirts. When working on this book, I decided to make a quilt of many different shirts. I used the wrong side of the blue fabric for the joining strips on the back of the quilt to highlight the dark blue blocks. If this feels uncomfortable to you, use the right side.

This project uses Joining Technique 3 (page 13) to piece the layers at the same time. The blocks will be attached with a wide front strip and a narrower back strip. Since you are quilting the block as you complete, there is no need for additional quilting.

FABRIC REQUIREMENTS

	Color		Yards	Inches	Centimeters
Fabric A		Dark Blue Cotton	4½ yds	156"	396.2cm

SUPPLIES

- Several shirts or other clothing of like weight
- 40" x 70" (101.6 x 177.8cm) extra-loft batting
- 2 spools dark blue thread
- Needed tools (page 9)

CUTTING INSTRUCTIONS

	Amount Needed	Use
Fabric A	(30) 7" x 10" (17.8 x 25.4cm) strips	backing fabric
	(60) 2½" x 4" (6.4 x 10.2cm) strips	
	(30) 3½" x 10" (8.9 x 25.4cm) strips	
	(24) 2" x 11" (5.1 x 27.9cm) strips	wide front strip
	(24) 1" x 11" (2.5 x 27.9cm) strips	narrow back strip
	(5) 2" x 40" (5.1 x 101.6cm) strips	wide front strip
	(5) 1" x 40" (2.5 x 101.6cm) strips	narrow back strip
	(1) 24" x 24" (61 x 61cm) square	bias tape
Shirts	(90) 2½" x 4" (6.4 x 10.2cm) strips	
Batting	(30) 7" x 10" (17.8 x 25.4cm) strips	

I also made "Eddy Bears" from my father's old shirts.

INSTRUCTIONS

1. Pin 7" x 10" (17.8 x 25.4cm) Fabric A strip to the batting, wrong side down, so the pieces stay in place as you piece the front. Flip the batting.

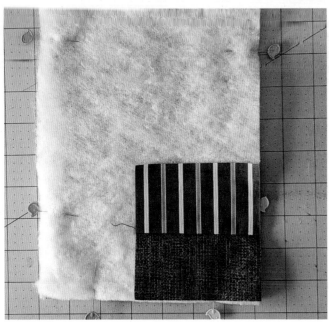

2. Pin one 2¼" x 4" (5.7 x 10.2cm) Fabric A strip in the bottom-right corner of the batting, as shown. Pin one shirt piece on top of the blue fabric, right sides together. Stitch along the top edge. Flip the fabric open and press the seam flat.

3. Pin another shirt piece to the one just sewn, right sides together. Stitch along the edge at the top as shown. Flip the fabric open and press the seam flat. Repeat with another shirt piece.

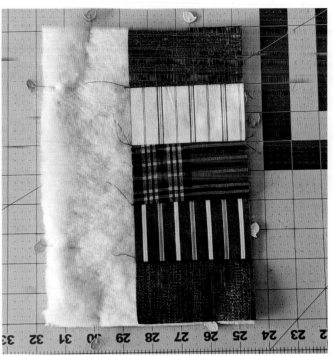

4. Pin and stitch another 2¼" x 4" (5.7 x 10.2cm) Fabric A strip to the one just sewn, right sides together. When flipped back and ironed, this completes the strip column.

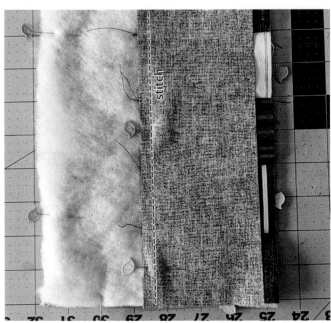

5. Pin the 3½" x 10" (8.9 x 25.4cm) Fabric A strip along the left side of the strip column, as shown. Stitch this strip in place. Flip back and press the seam flat.

6. Quilt the block according to the diagram. Square the block to 7" x 10" (17.8 x 25.4cm).

7. Repeat steps 1–6 to make 29 more blocks.

ASSEMBLY & FINISHING

8. Lay out the blocks according to the diagram, arranging the shirt designs in the order that you want.

Memory Quilt | **123**

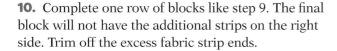

9. Using Technique 3, join the first and second blocks using 2" x 11" (5.1 x 27.9cm) Fabric A strips and 1" x 11" (2.5 x 27.9cm) Fabric A strips. When attaching the 1" x 11" (2.5 x 27.9cm) strips, pin the wrong side down; this will create a light blue strip on the back, showing the wrong side of the fabric. If desired, place as normal for a dark blue strip.

10. Complete one row of blocks like step 9. The final block will not have the additional strips on the right side. Trim off the excess fabric strip ends.

11. Using Technique 3, join the rows using 2" x 40" (5.1 x 101.6cm) Fabric A strips and 1" x 40" (2.5 x 101.6cm) Fabric A strips.

12. Use the 24" x 24" (61 x 61cm) Fabric A square to make ½" (1.2cm) double-fold bias tape (page 16). Attach the bias tape around the outside of the quilt.

Memory quilts are great to make something functional from beloved fabrics, but you can also make this into a piece for display.

Photo Album Wrap

Just like the Memory Quilt, this memory album is a great gift for a grieving friend or family member. It can be made of any recycled or new fabrics for a special gift.

FABRIC REQUIREMENTS

	Color		Yards	Inches	Centimeters
Fabric A		Dark Blue Cotton	¼ yd	9"	22.9cm
Shirts		Plaid and striped		Remnants	

SUPPLIES

- (2) 9" x 10½" (22.9 x 26.7cm) batting
- Dark blue thread
- Quilt basting spray
- Needed tools (page 9)

CUTTING INSTRUCTIONS

	Amount Needed	Use
Fabric A	(2) 3¼" x 9" (8.3 x 22.9cm) strips	
	(1) 2¼" x 11" (5.7 x 27.9cm) strip	pocket
	(2) 9" x 10½" (22.9 x 26.7cm) strips	backing fabric
Shirts	(2) 3¼" x 3½" (8.3 x 8.9cm) squares	
	(1) 3½" x 3½" (8.9 x 8.9cm) square	
	(2) 3¼" x 9" (8.3 x 22.9cm) strips	inside flap
	(1) 3½" x 9" (8.9 x 22.9cm) strip	inside flap
	(1) 2¼" x 11" (5.7 x 27.9cm) strip	pocket
	(2) 2" x 24" (5.1 x 61cm) strips	binding
	(1) 1½" x 9" (3.8 x 22.9cm) strip; button placket or other special fabric	detail (optional)

The wrap opens on the left side to easily slip onto the cover of any album.

Including the button placket adds a little detail that can remind you of the fabric's origin as a shirt.

FRONT OF THE WRAP

1. Spray one side of one batting with basting spray. Lay the sticky side of the batting onto the wrong side of 9" x 10½" (22.9 x 26.7cm) Fabric A strip. Flip the batting over.

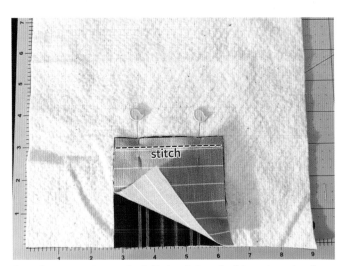

2. Place one 3¼" x 3½" (8.3 x 8.9cm) shirt piece in the bottom-center of the batting. The longest side should be along the bottom edge. Place 3½" x 3½" (8.9 x 8.9cm) shirt square on top of the first piece, right sides together, and stitch the seam on the top.

3. Stitch the remaining 3¼" x 3½" (8.3 x 8.9cm) shirt piece on top of the unit, aligning the 3½" (8.9cm) sides. Sew it to the batting.

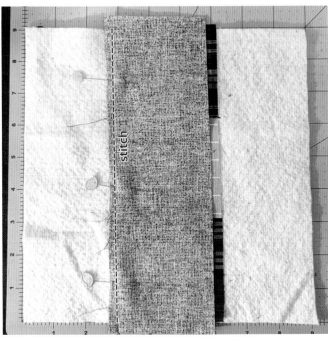

4. Stitch one 3¼" x 9" (8.3 x 22.9cm) Fabric A strip to the left side of the unit. Stitch the second same-size strip to the right side.

5. Quilt the blue strips as shown with straight lines ⅜" (1cm) apart.

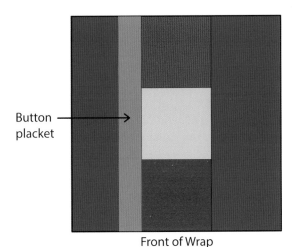

Button placket →

Front of Wrap

6. If desired, stitch the button placket on the left side of the center pieces for texture and depth. It will be on top of the Fabric A strip from step 4.

INSIDE FLAP OF THE WRAP

7. Repeat step 1 with the remaining batting and Fabric A piece.

Inside Flap

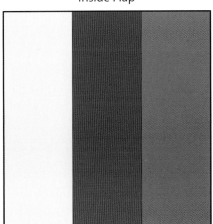

8. Place one 3¼" x 9" (8.3 x 22.9cm) shirt strip along one edge of the batting. Place the 3½" x 9" (8.9 x 22.9cm) shirt strip on top of the first and stitch in place. Flip back and press. Repeat with the remaining 3¼" x 9" (8.3 x 22.9cm) shirt strip.

9. Stitch the 2¼" x 11" (5.7 x 27.9cm) shirt strip to the 2¼" x 11" (5.7 x 27.9cm) Fabric A strip, right sides together. Press the seam open. Stitch a ½" (1.3cm) hem on the long edge of the shirt strip. This is the pocket.

Inside flap

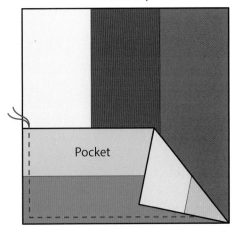

Pocket

10. Lay the pocket, right side up, on the unit from step 8. Stitch the sides and bottom of the pocket to complete the inside flap of the wrap.

ASSEMBLY & FINISHING

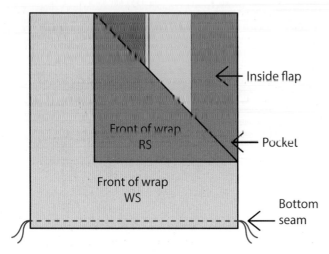

11. Place the front of the wrap on top of the inside flap, right sides together. Turn 90 degrees counterclockwise. The bottom edge is where the seam needs to be; mark this edge if you need to. Stitch the two blocks together. Press the seam open.

12. Fold one of the 2" x 24" (5.1 x 61cm) shirt strips in half and press. Open and fold the two ends to the center crease. Press the two new folds. Fold this strip in half again and press. This is a ½" (1.3cm) double-fold bias tape (page 14) that is not cut on the bias. Repeat with the second strip.

13. Unfold the wrap as shown below. Stitch one bias tape to the outside of the wrap of one short ends. Using the other bias tape, stitch the other short end. Use one to cover the bottom seam that joins the front of the wrap and the inside flap. Using the remaining bias tape, stitch one to each of the long edges.

14. Bring the right sides together again. Stitch the long edges along the bias tape. Flip inside out, and slide the completed wrap onto the photo album.

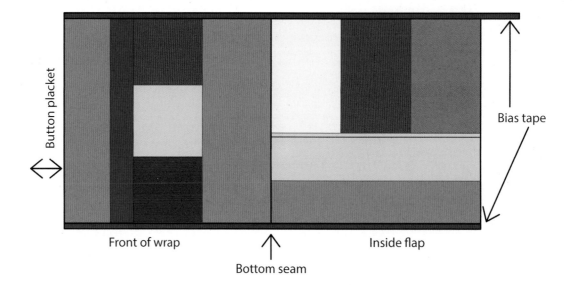

My recommendation is to match the special fabrics to a photo album of that person, to make a collection of memories

Crazy Quilt Pillow

I love crazy quilting! I find it to be relaxing and a terrific way to thin out my quilting and sewing stash. If you have never done crazy quilting, we will just touch the basics. There are really no rules. The method is simply to stitch, flip, and press the seams.

SUPPLIES

- Fabric scraps of all kinds; I used scraps from all the projects in this book
- 16" x 16" (40.6 x 40.6cm) backing fabric
- (4) 8" x 8" (20.3 x 20.3cm) needled cotton batting
- Assorted thread, if machine embroidering
- Assorted floss and needle, if hand embroidering
- Small charms, flowers, buttons, and other tiny baubles (optional)
- 16" x 16" (40.6 x 40.6cm) pillow form
- Needed tools (page 9)

CHAPTER TWELVE: BOOK SCRAP PROJECTS

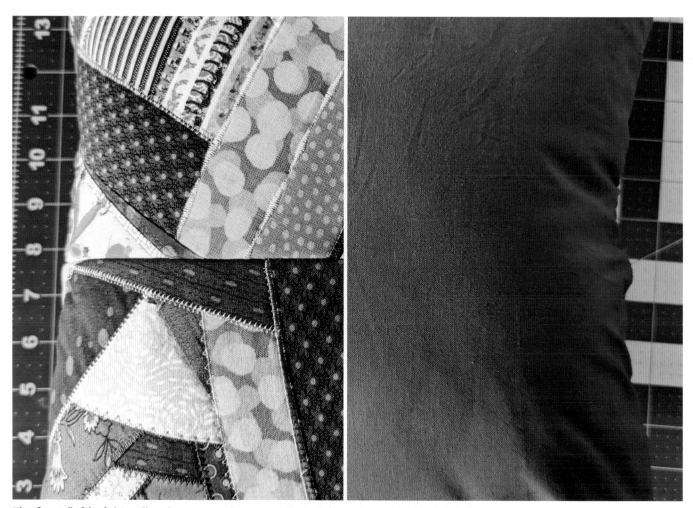

The front (left) of this pillow has so much interest that I left the back (right) plain to not distract.

INSTRUCTIONS

1. Make a center piece for the crazy quilt. Usually, crazy quilting starts with a pentagon (five-sided shape). This keeps the pattern flowing out from the center, but you can use your imagination and start in a corner, use a triangle, or try other multisided shapes.

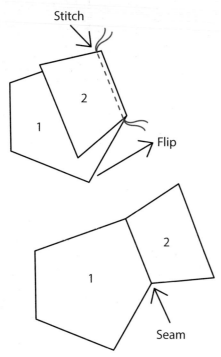

2. Place the center piece on the batting. Place a scrap on top, right sides together, that is close to the same length. Stitch them together to the batting. Flip the fabric back and press the seam open.

3. Turn the block slightly and work the same way with another piece of fabric. Remember to use one about the same length as the new side. Stitch. Flip the fabric back and press the seam open.

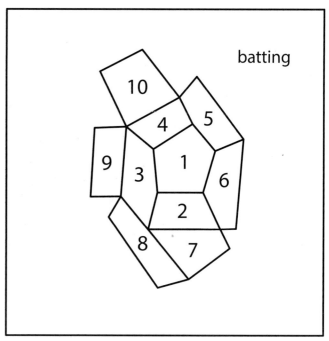

4. Continue in this manner by rotating the block after each piece is added. Plan your own pattern by colors or attack this project with random colors.

5. When the entire piece of batting is covered, trim the excess from the batting. Repeat to make three more blocks.

6. Stitch two blocks, right sides together. Stitch the other two blocks together. Join the two rows together, matching seams. This is the front of the pillow.

7. Either use your sewing machine to embroider random designs on the patchwork along the seams or embroider by hand with floss. For a more distinct crazy quilt piece, add small charms, flowers, buttons, and other tiny baubles.

ASSEMBLY & FINISHING

8. Stitch the pillow front and the backing fabric, right sides together. Leave 7" (17.8cm) open and unstitched. There is no batting on the back of the pillow.

9. Clip the corners. Turn the pillow inside out, push out the corners from inside, and press the seams to square the pillow cover.

10. Slide the pillow form into the pillow cover and maneuver to fill the corners and sides evenly. Hand stitch the opening shut.

Crumb Quilt Pillow & Wrap

FINISHED SIZE: 12" x 20" (30.5 x 50.8cm)

I love crumb quilting as much as crazy quilting. They are so similar but with vastly different finished looks. Crumb quilts are usually made of lines of scraps, often squares and rectangles. Any piece of scrap fabric can be used. The fabrics are joined in a chain of seamed pieces that can then be trimmed for straight edges or used with rough, raw edges. We are going to sew them to the batting in narrow columns, so we don't have to stop and add the backing and batting later. This technique is a fantastic way to use scraps. Don't throw anything away!

FABRIC REQUIREMENTS

	Color	Yards	Inches	Centimeters
Fabric A	Black and White Striped	1 yd	36"	91.4cm

SUPPLIES

- Fabric scraps of all kinds; I used scraps from all the projects in this book
- 8" x 23" (20.3 x 58.4cm) needled cotton batting
- 48" (121.9cm) twill tape, ⅝" (1.6cm) wide
- 12" x 20" (30.5 x 50.8cm) pillow form
- Needed tools (page 9)

CUTTING INSTRUCTIONS

	Amount Needed	Use
Fabric A	(1) 8" x 23" (20.3 x 58.4cm) strip	backing fabric
	(2) 12" x 20" (30.5 x 50.8cm) strips	pillow
	(3) 2" x 25" (5.1 x 63.5cm) strips	bias tape
Twill Tape	(4) 12" (30.5cm) strips	

PILLOW

1. Stitch the two 12" x 20" (30.5 x 50.8cm) Fabric A and stitch around the edge with a ¼" (6.4mm) seam allowance, leaving a 6" (15.2cm) opening for turrning. Clip the corners.

2. Flip the pillow cover inside out and push out all corners and seams. Insert the pillow form and maneuver it to lay evenly in the corners and sides. Hand stitch the opening closed. Set it aside.

PILLOW WRAP

3. Draw three lines down the long side of the batting, 2" (5.1cm) apart. There will be four 23" (58.4cm) long columns.

4. Place a scrap of fabric at the bottom of the first column. Place another on top of the first, right sides together, and stitch at the top. Flip the fabric back to the batting and press as in the Crazy Quilt Pillow. Repeat with scraps to fill this column. Only stitch between the batting edge and the first line. Trim the fabrics along the line.

5. Complete the other three columns in the same manner, keeping the fabrics trimmed to the lines.

6. Fold one 2" x 25" (5.1 x 63.5cm) Fabric A strip in half lengthwise and press the fold. Open the strip and fold the sides into the center crease. Press the two new folds. This is a 1" (2.5cm) single-fold bias tape that is not cut on the bias (page 17). Repeat with the other two Fabric A strips.

7. Pin and stitch the bias tape down the length of crumb quilt where the lines are positioned. Stitch on both sides of the bias, close to the edge. Trim the bias tape ends.

ASSEMBLY & FINISHING

8. Pin the pieced front and 8" x 23" (20.3 x 58.4cm) Fabric A strip, right sides together. Pin the bias ends so they will catch in the seam.

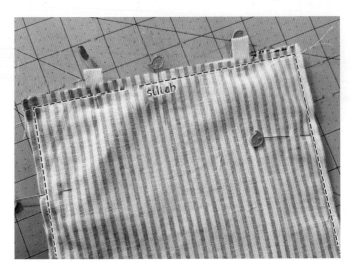

9. Place two lengths of twill tape in between the batting and backing fabric. Place both on one short end with ⅛" (3.2mm) showing beyond the seam line. Line up with the first and third bias tape. Stitch around the pillow cover, catching the bias tape edges and the twill ends. Leave 7" (17.8cm) open for turning right side out.

10. Clip the corners. Flip the wrap right out and shape. Hand stitch the opening closed.

11. Fold the wrap around the striped lumbar pillow and tie the twill.

Templates

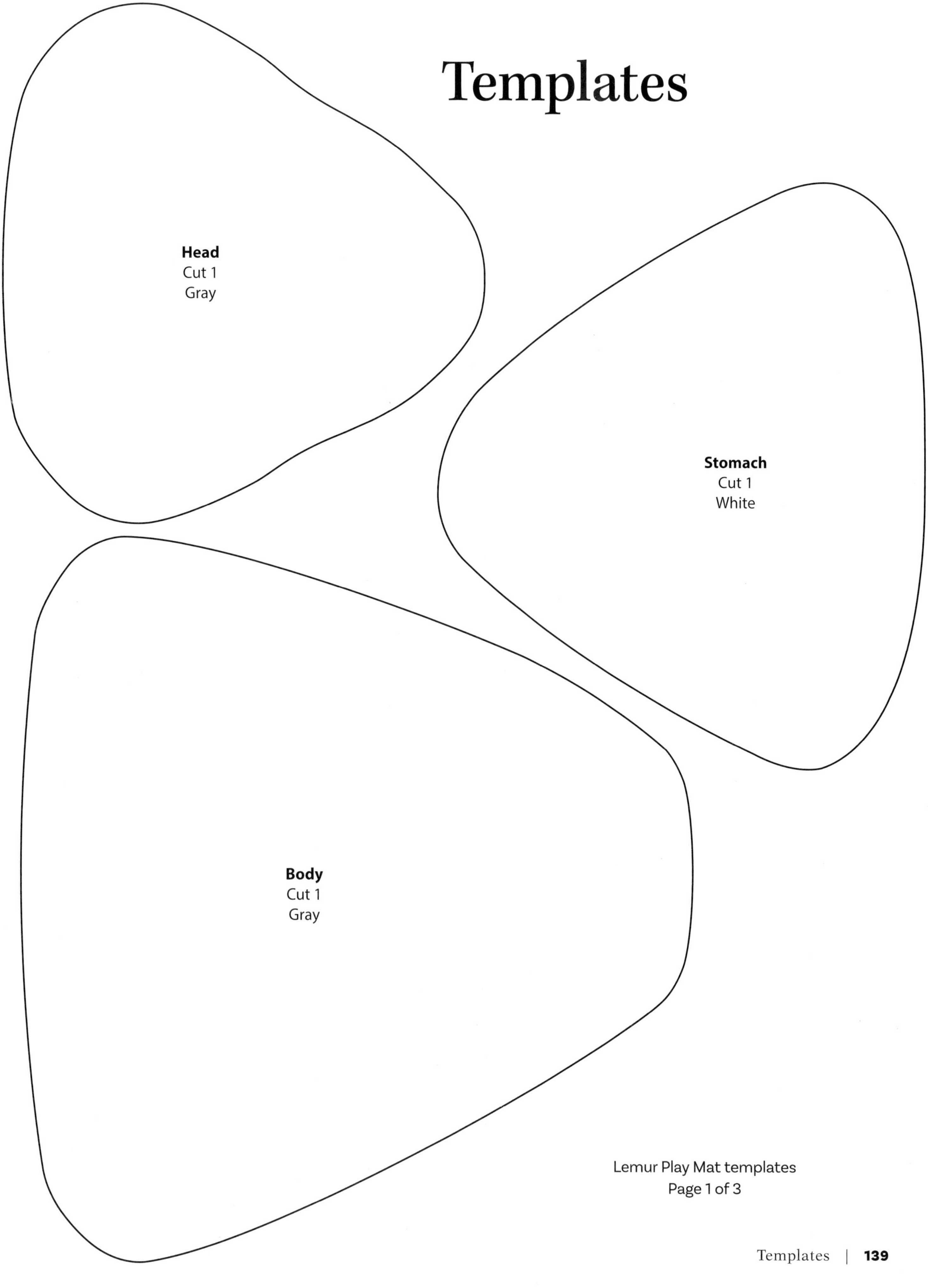

Head
Cut 1
Gray

Stomach
Cut 1
White

Body
Cut 1
Gray

Lemur Play Mat templates
Page 1 of 3

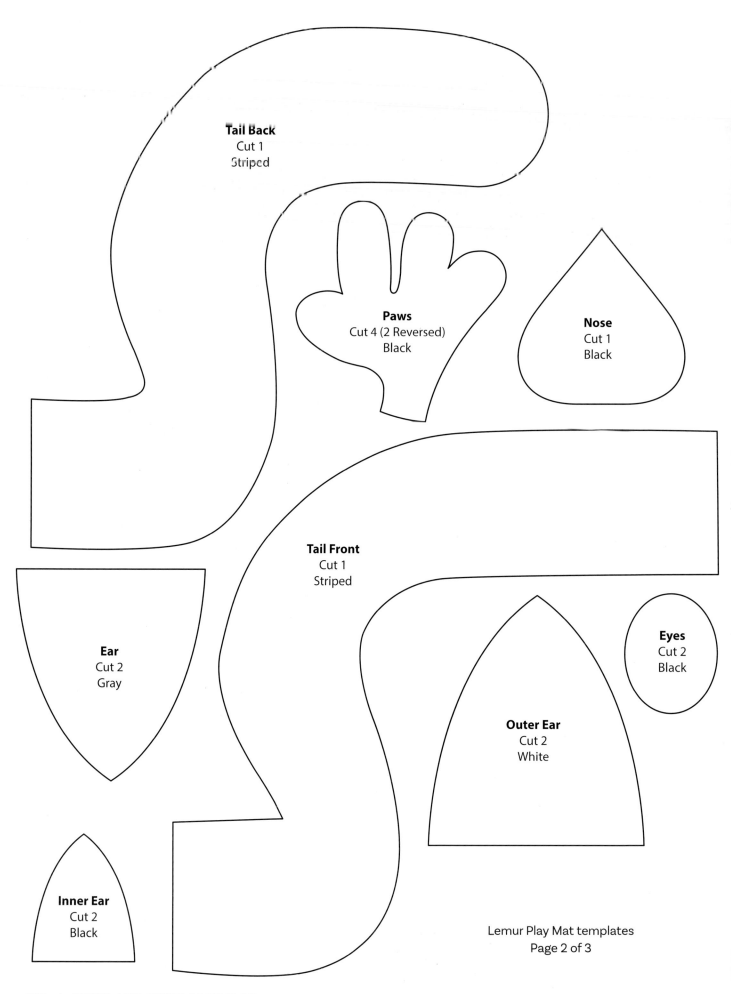

Tail Back
Cut 1
Striped

Paws
Cut 4 (2 Reversed)
Black

Nose
Cut 1
Black

Tail Front
Cut 1
Striped

Ear
Cut 2
Gray

Outer Ear
Cut 2
White

Eyes
Cut 2
Black

Inner Ear
Cut 2
Black

Lemur Play Mat templates
Page 2 of 3

Face
Cut 1
White

Balloon
Cut 3
White

Lemur Play Mat templates
Page 3 of 3

About the Author

Debi Schmitz-Noriega has been a professional designer for over 35 years and a lifelong creator. With hundreds of tear sheets and magazine designs, she has also appeared on television and has authored numerous craft books.

Debi earned her stripes in the craft industry and is known as one of the "seasoned professionals." Many of her designs have been featured in online magazines, manufacturer websites, advertisements, and at multiple trade shows across the country. She fervently follows worldwide trends to introduce new products for the craft, home décor, fashion, and quilt industries.

Debi has experience at the retail, wholesale, manufacturing, and import level. Her accomplishments include designing product catalogues, patterns for marketing, product packaging, and kits for many manufacturers.

Debi has an engaging personality that exudes her enthusiasm about products. She loves teaching and demonstrating her talents. Debi and her husband, Jaime, have six grown children and ten grandchildren between them. Her passion for product and design is only surpassed by her faith and her love of family, friends, pets, and her home state of Iowa.

Special Thanks

Thank you for the following products:

AccuQuilt: GO! Me® Fabric Cutter and Die #55012
Website: https://www.accuquilt.com/

Coats: Dual Duty thread
Website: https://www.coats.com/en/products/threads/dual-duty/dual-duty

Crazy Redhead Quilting (Newton, Iowa): Quilt shop
*I'd like to thank Laura for taking the time to introduce
me to my Brother sewing machine. I love it!*
Website: https://www.crazyredheadquilting.com/

Fairfield: Poly-Fil Extra-Loft® Batting
Website: https://shop.fairfieldworld.com/product-category/batting/

Mary Ellen Products: Best Press Starch and Sizing Alternative
Website: https://www.maryellenproducts.com/

P. Carter Carpin: Fabrics
Etsy: https://www.etsy.com/shop/pcartercarpin
Facebook: https://www.facebook.com/PCarterCarpinsSeriousWhimsey/

Sue Penn: Fabrics
Website: https://freespiritfabrics.com/sue-penn-collections/
Facebook: https://www.facebook.com/suepenndesigns/

Therm O Web: Basting spray, iron-on adhesive, and iron-on sewing
tape adhesive
Website: https://www.thermoweb.com/

The Warm Company: Warm & Natural® Needled Cotton Batting
Website: https://warmcompany.com/

Index